D1155880

Ready-to-Use

SELF-ESTEEM ACTIVITIES

FOR SECONDARY STUDENTS
...PECIAL NEEDS

...LENE MANNIX

...tions by Tim Mannix

THE CENTER FOR APPLIED
RESEARCH IN EDUCATION
West Nyack, New York 10994

Library of Congress Cataloging-in-Publication Data

Mannix, Darlene.
Ready-to-use self-esteem activities for secondary students with special needs / Darlene Mannix ; illustrations by Tim Mannix.
p. cm.
ISBN 0-87628-758-5 (spiral-wire). — ISBN 0-87628-887-5 (pbk.)
1. Handicapped youth—Education (Secondary)—United States.
2. Self-esteem—Study and teaching (Secondary)—United States.
3. Activity programs in education—United States. I. Title.
LC4019.M26 1996
371.91—dc20 96-9694
CIP

Printed in the United States of America

10 9 8 7 6 5 4 3 2 1

ISBN 0-87628-887-5 (P) ISBN 0-87628-758-5 (S)

THE CENTER FOR APPLIED RESEARCH IN EDUCATION
West Nyack, NY 10994
A Simon & Schuster Company

On the World Wide Web at http://www.phdirect.com

Prentice Hall International (UK) Limited, *London*
Prentice Hall of Australia Pty. Limited, *Sydney*
Prentice Hall Canada, Inc., *Toronto*
Prentice Hall Hispanoamericana, S.A., *Mexico*
Prentice Hall of India Private Limited, *New Delhi*
Prentice Hall of Japan, Inc., *Tokyo*
Simon & Schuster Asia Pte. Ltd., *Singapore*
Editora Prentice Hall do Brasil, Ltda., *Rio de Janeiro*

This book is dedicated affectionately to my good friends at Horse Master Stable:

Cookie and Steve Ferguson
Jo Rooksby
Larry, Ellen, and Jeff Toll
Linn and Lauren George
Susan O'Brien
Ron, Hollis, and Jean Oselka
Chris Sulewski
Erin and Jan Claeys
Jennifer Mannix
Crystal & Jordan

About the Author

Darlene Mannix has been a teacher in public and private schools for the past seventeen years where she has worked with students of all ages who are at-risk, language disordered, and emotionally, mentally and learning disabled. She has also taught alternative education classes for middle school students.

Ms. Mannix holds a Bachelor of Science degree from Taylor University and a Master's in Learning Disabilities from Indiana University. She is an active member of the Council for Exceptional Children.

Ms. Mannix is the author of several books published by The Center for Applied Research in Education: *Oral Language Activities for Special Children* (1987), *Be a Better Student: Lessons and Worksheets for Teaching Behavior Management in Grades 4-9* (1989), *Life Skills Activities for Special Children* (1991), *Social Skills Activities for Special Children* (1993), and *Life Skills Activities for Secondary Students with Special Needs* (1995). She is also the author of several workbooks published with other companies that deal with reading, behavior management, and forms for teachers.

About This Book

Ready-to-Use Self-Esteem Activities for Secondary Students with Special Needs is a workbook for both teachers and students. The materials are appropriate for resource settings, individual counseling sessions, use with small groups, and even for an entire class or theme-directed units.

The material is organized into four main sections:

- Part I is entitled *What Is Self-Esteem?* This section, composed of eight lessons and 16 ready-to-use worksheets, deals with vocabulary, the ups and downs of self-esteem, evaluating self-esteem, and much more!

  Included in each lesson is at least one learning objective, introductory activities, at least one student worksheet, several discussion questions about and extending from the worksheets, lesson review questions, journal-entry ideas for both student and teacher, and a personal goal for the day for the teacher.

  After completing this section, the student should have a good understanding of what is commonly meant by "self-esteem" and have an appreciation of why this is important.

- Part II, *Factors That Affect Self-Esteem,* explains and discusses factors that can affect how an individual develops his or her self-esteem. The effect of important people such as family members, friends, and peer groups are discussed, as well as other factors including life experiences, individual talent and abilities, and values. There are nine lessons and 21 ready-to-use worksheets in this section.

  The format of these lessons is similar to the first section, in that each lesson includes at least one objective, introductory activities, student worksheets, discussion questions, lesson review questions, journal-entry ideas, and a daily personal goal for the teacher.

  Upon completing this section, the student will have been exposed to and have considered many different factors that contribute to shaping one's self-esteem.

- Part III focuses on *Combatting a Low Self-Esteem.* This is a collection of 22 lessons and 24 ready-to-use worksheets that deal with interventions for a specific emotion or feeling. These lessons can be completed in any order or selected as necessary.

  The format for these lessons is a little different from the previous two sections. Each lesson begins with behavioral examples of the low self-esteem, possible reasons why an individual might feel this way about him- or herself, a case study, and ideas for the student, teacher, and parent to try to improve the situation. There are also three specific activities for each lesson: discussion of the case study, ways to personalize the lesson for individual student use, and a general worksheet for use by all students. Also included are journal-entry ideas for the student.

  After completing the lessons in Part III, the student should be able to generate several ideas for combatting each specific aspect of a low self-esteem.

- Part IV is entitled *Building a Healthy Self-Esteem.* The 22 lessons and accompanying worksheets in this section focus on developing characteristics of successful, healthy people. Tips are given for evaluating one's own self-esteem for the purpose of becoming more insightful and practicing good mental and physical health.

The format for these lessons is similar to Part III, in that each opens with examples of positive self-esteem behavior; a desired outcome; a case study; ideas to try for the student, teacher, and parent; and three activities: examination of the case study, personal application activities, and a student worksheet. Discussion questions and journal-entry ideas are also included.

After working through the activities in Part IV, the student will easily recognize characteristics and comments of an individual with a healthy self-esteem and be able to identify specific ways to incorporate these healthy characteristics into his or her own lifestyle.

Ready-to-Use Self-Esteem Activities for Secondary Students with Special Needs is a resource for educators, counselors, parents, and others who are interested and involved in helping students with special needs. *All* students must be helped to develop a positive self-concept and healthy self-esteem. This book will help you do that!

Darlene Mannix

Table of Contents

Part I

What Is Self-Esteem?

In this section you'll find eight lessons and sixteen ready-to-use worksheets that provide your students with a sound understanding of what is commonly meant by "self-esteem" and why it is important. "Valuing Something," "Rating Your Self-Esteem," and "The Ups and Downs of Self-Esteem" are just a sample of the introductory lessons that lay the groundwork for the rest of the lessons and activities in this resource.

Lesson 1: Important Definitions

Students may not have a clear idea of what self-esteem consists of. There are many terms relating to the self that are used interchangeably and may need some clarification. What is self-image? self-confidence? self-concept? self-control? self-esteem? In order to lay the basis for the ideas and instruction in this book, the student and teacher must each understand these terms and how they affect self-esteem.

Objective

- The student will explain the difference between **self-concept** and **self-esteem.**
- The student will distinguish between examples of characteristics of self-concept (physical attributes, abilities, etc.) and self-esteem (placing value).

Introduction

1. Ask students to list as many terms as they can think of that begin with the prefix "self" (*self-confidence, self-reliant, etc.*).
2. Briefly define the terms as a class by writing a simple definition next to each term.

Examples: self-reliant — able to do things on your own
self-confidence — sure of yourself
self-respect — treating yourself with pride
self-concept — what you think of yourself
self-esteem — how you value yourself
self-directed — able to motivate yourself
self-image — the picture you have of yourself

3. Put a * next to self-concept and self-esteem. Explain that you are going to concentrate on these two terms in this lesson.

Worksheet #1: Self-Concept and Self-Esteem

Synopsis: Self-concept is a collection of ideas and beliefs that an individual has about himself or herself. Self-esteem takes those beliefs and assigns or places worth or value upon them.

Directions: Have students read the paragraphs on the worksheet about self-concept and self-esteem. Then either individually or as a group, have students complete the discussion questions and review questions.

Answers (examples):

Discussion Questions

1. probably comments about what the person looks like; perhaps personality traits, accomplishments, etc.
2. probably most people are somewhat in tune with their abilities, characteristics, and physical appearance
3. eye color, hair color, skin color, physical abilities

Review Questions

1. facts and beliefs about oneself
2. the value placed upon oneself
3. someone may not value those characteristics about himself or herself

WORKSHEET #2: SELF-CONCEPT STATEMENTS

Synopsis: Some self-concept statements are based on facts (physical characteristics, proven accomplishments, etc.) and others are based on beliefs (that may or may not be true).

Directions: Students are to read the self-concept statements on the worksheet and decide whether they are based on a fact or a belief.

Answers:

1. belief; 2. fact; 3. fact; 4. fact; 5. belief; 6. belief; 7. fact; 8. belief; 9. belief; 10. belief

Discussion:

1. Look over the statements you marked as a "fact." What proof could be given to substantiate each comment?
2. Look over the statements you marked as a "belief." What type of proof could be found to change it to a fact?
3. Do you think most people are accurate when it comes to describing themselves?

WORKSHEET #3: SELF-ESTEEM STATEMENTS

Synopsis: When something is held in high esteem, it is valued by the individual. Different individuals may value different things.

Directions: Students are to read comments given by individuals on the worksheet and to decide, based on the comments, what specifically is valued by that individual.

Answers:

1. hair color; 2. tennis ability; 3. ability to solve math problems; 4. friendship, specifically a best friend; 5. attendance at work

Discussion:

1. What type of clues were given in each case on the worksheet to tip you off as to what the individual valued? (*emotional reaction to hair color, pride in tennis ability, frustration over math, etc.*)
2. What phrases in each example give a clue as to how strongly the person feels about what is valued? (*I hate . . . ; no one can beat me . . . ; it doesn't matter . . . ; nothing is more important . . . ; I think it's important . . .*)

LESSON REVIEW

1. What is meant by self-concept?
2. What is meant by self-esteem?
3. Give an example of a comment that indicates a good self-concept.
4. Give an example of a comment that indicates a good self-esteem.

JOURNAL-ENTRY IDEAS

- Self-concept is a collection of facts and ideas about yourself. Describe yourself in your journal. What do you believe to be true about yourself?
- Self-esteem involves placing worth or value upon yourself. Make a list of characteristics you think are important in a person. Place a * next to those that you believe you possess.
- Think about a time when you were really proud of yourself. What did you do? What were the circumstances?
- Write about what you were like in the first or second grade. How did you feel about yourself, your life, your family, etc., back then?

- How are you different now from the child you were in first or second grade? What has happened to cause those changes? Do you think you were happier back then or right now? Why or why not?

Teacher Journal

It can be an awesome responsibility to know you are in some way responsible for and influential on the development of the self-esteem of your students. What do you see as you look over the bodies sitting at the desks in your classroom?

Goal for the Day

Today I will listen for comments my students make that reflect their opinion of their self-concept and self-esteem. I will write down what I hear and think about the types of comments being made.

Name______________________________ Date ______________

Self-Concept and Self-Esteem

Worksheet #1

Directions: Read the following paragraphs about self-concept and self-esteem. Then answer the questions that follow.

Self-esteem is not quite the same thing as self-concept or self-image. Let's take a look at what these terms mean.

Pretend you are looking into a mirror. What do you see? Perhaps you see a face with blue eyes, tanned skin, and dark hair. What do you think other people see when they look at you? Maybe they see someone who helps other people, or someone who is a good artist. When someone comes up to you and asks you to tell about yourself, what information do you give? You might say that you are a student, that you work part-time at a bike repair shop, and that you have four sisters and a dog. All of these bits of information are part of what makes up the image or concept of you.

Your self-concept is simply a collection of the facts and beliefs you have about yourself. You might think you are tall until you stand next to a professional basketball player and find that your neck hurts! Your self-concept changes as you do. When you were young, perhaps you believed you could beat up burglars and ride your bike across the state. As you grew older, you realized you have limitations as well as strengths that you weren't aware of before.

Self-esteem takes the self-concept you have developed and decides how much you like or approve of it. It places value or worth upon your self-concept.

Maybe a person believes he is smart, good-looking, and the most popular person in school. You would think he would have a good self-concept. But suppose the most important thing to him is being a good athlete. Even though he has some desirable qualities, he may always feel that he is not good enough at something that is important to him. He may dread going to P.E. class or try to avoid joining any sports teams because he knows he will be a failure.

It is important to have a good self-concept and a high self esteem. More about that later!

Discussion Questions

1. If you walked up to someone and asked him or her to describe him- or herself, what types of comments do you think the person would make? Why?

___

___

___

2. Do you think most people are honest with themselves and others about their comments about themselves?

___

___

___

3. What are some characteristics people are born with?

___

___

___

Review Questions

1. What is meant by self-concept?

___

___

___

2. What is meant by self-esteem?

___

___

___

3. How could someone have a lot of good qualities yet still have a low self-esteem?

___

___

___

___

Name____ Date ____________

Self-Concept Statements

Worksheet #2

Directions: Read the following comments of students about themselves. Tell whether the statement is based on a **fact** or a **belief** about himself or herself.

1. I am really good-looking. ____________

2. I weigh about 20 pounds more than I should for my height, according to the chart that my doctor gave me. ____________

3. Last summer, I played shortstop on the city's softball team. ____________

4. I am an African-American. ____________

5. I think I am the tallest girl in the class. ____________

6. I have a bad temper when people irritate me. ____________

7. My eyes are bluish-green. ____________

8. I am probably the fastest runner on the track team. ____________

9. I have a lot of friends. ____________

10. People always tell me that I have a really nice smile. ____________

Name______________________________ Date ____________

Self-Esteem Statements

Worksheet #

Directions: The following comments indicate something about the self-esteem of the studen[t]. Remember, to esteem something means to place some value upon something. For each statement belo[w] decide what is valued for each student.

1. I have bright red hair. Everyone assumes that if you have red hair, you also have a bad temper. I hate my hair. I would do anything to change it.

   ____

   ____

2. No one can beat me at tennis. I have taken lessons for years and finally I can beat my instructor nearly every time we play. I love to be challenged by people who don't know me — it just gives me another chance to prove how good I am!

   ____

   ____

3. It doesn't matter how many times I re-do this math assignment; I know it will still be wrong. I just can't seem to understand how to work those kinds of problems.

   ____

   ____

4. There is nothing more important than having a best friend. It doesn't matter how many acquaintances you have, as long as you know there is one person whom you can count on.

   ____

   ____

5. I take pride in the fact that I have not missed a day of work in two years. I think it is important to show up when there is work to be done. My boss knows that she can count on me.

   ____

   ____

Lesson 2: Valuing Something

Everyone values something. It may be a possession, a quality in another person, or perhaps an acquired skill. In this lesson, the activities focus on having the student pick out something that is valued by another person and finally begin to think about things that are valued by him- or herself.

Objectives

- Given specific situations, the student will be able to state items or qualities that are valued by others.
- The student will list several items or qualities that are important to him or her.

Introduction

List the names of several celebrities on the board. Have students think of something that would probably be valued or important to that person. (For example, a rock star may value a good guitar, a politician may value his voters, a sports celebrity may value fame or money, etc.) Ask students to give facts or some evidence for their opinions.

WORKSHEET #4: WHAT SOMEONE ESTEEMS

Synopsis: Individuals may value an item that represents achievement, a pet, the attainment of a goal, or a quality in another person. There are different reasons why people value what they do.

Directions: Have students read the paragraphs about students who value different things. Then have them answer the discussion questions.

Answers (examples):

1. Tomas – trophy; Alison – dog; Jessie – items from her mother
2. disappointed in his father, angry over the loss of the trophy
3. she waited a long time for the dog
4. The objects themselves may have some value (necklace), but most likely Jessie places value on the objects because they belonged to her mother.

WORKSHEET #5: LEARNING TO VALUE SOMETHING

Synopsis: Individuals may place different amounts of value on the same item or quality. What is extremely important or valuable to one person may have little importance to another. There is a lot of relativity in valuing something!

Directions: Students are to rank the students on the worksheet in order according to how much they probably value the item or quality on the worksheet situations.

Answers:

1. José, Jeff, Amy; 2. Tony, Ramona, Sam; 3. Louis, Carla, Malisa

Discussion:

1. What was your basis for ranking the students in item #1? (*amount of time spent in the sport*)
2. How did you decide who valued good grades the most? (*the one who spent the most time working for them*)
3. What are some situations in which Louis's honesty might not be welcomed? (*when he should be polite instead of blunt*)
4. Do you think Carla is wrong to lie to her friend? (*the situation may be resolved by Carla conveying her feelings to her friend in a gentle way rather than by lying to her*)

Worksheet #6: What Is Important to You?

Synopsis: Individuals may value different sorts of things. It is important to think about possessions, qualities, people, and other things that are personally valued and perhaps the reasons why they are of personal value.

Directions: Students are to read the suggested items on the list and check the ones that are important or valuable to them. Students are encouraged to add other items to the list.

Discussion:

1. Are there certain items or qualities you think are valued by almost any person? (*honesty, money, gold, friendship, etc.*) Why?
2. When you think about what is important to you, do you have to think awhile or is it easy to select things?
3. Have the things on your list today changed from what you would have valued several years ago? Do you think the items will be different several years from now?

Lesson Review

1. What is an example of a possession that might be valued by someone?
2. What is an example of an ability or skill that might be valued by someone?
3. What is an example of a personal quality that might be valued by someone?

Journal-Entry Ideas

- What is a possession you particularly value? How did you obtain it? Where do you keep it? Why is it valuable to you?
- Think about your best friend. What is one particular quality you really admire about your best friend? Write about a circumstance in which your friend demonstrated this quality.
- If you could have a new skill, talent, or ability, what would it be? Who is someone who possesses this ability?

Teacher Journal

Look around your desk. What items have you placed there? A picture of your son or daughter? A paperweight from a student last year? Why do you treasure these items?

Goal for the Day

Today I will ask several students about something that is of value to them. Perhaps it will be obvious—a ring, a football, some other item. But I will dig a little deeper for some other students. I will try to ascertain what that quiet student in the back values.

Name____ Date ______________

What Someone Esteems

Worksheet #4

Directions: Read the following paragraphs about what it means to esteem, or value, something. Then answer the questions.

Tomas worked all season to improve his skills at baseball. By the end of the season, Tomas was awarded a trophy for the most improved player. As he walked up in front of his teammates to receive it, he was proud of himself for this achievement. The applause was wonderful. He could hardly believe that this time the trophy was going to him.

Alison had wanted a dog for as long as she could remember, but having a sister with allergies made this seem like an impossible dream. The day finally came when her sister finished school, got a job, and moved out of the house. Alison went to the animal shelter the next day and picked out the homeliest mutt she could find. She loved her new pal!

Jessie's mother was killed in a car accident when Jessie was very young. She didn't remember much about her mother, but always wished she could find out what she was like. On her sixteenth birthday, Jessie's aunt gave Jessie a necklace that had belonged to her mother and an old photo album that contained pictures of Jessie and her mother.

Discussion Questions:

1. What is valued by each of the individuals in the paragraphs?

____

____

2. How do you think Tomas would feel if his father tossed the trophy out into the garbage?

____

____

3. Why do you think Alison values having a dog so much?

____

____

4. Do you think Jessie values the objects given to her by her aunt only because her mother is not living? Why else might she value them?

____

____

Name____ Date ______________

Learning to Value Something

Worksheet #5

Directions: Rank each of the three individuals below from lowest (1) to highest (3) according to how much each probably values the item or characteristic given.

1. ability to play soccer well

José practices with the soccer team every day after school and practices on his own with friends.

____

Amy doesn't like sports of any kind.

____

Jeff plays soccer for fun but he also likes to play softball.

____

2. good grades

Ramona's mother makes her go to a tutor every day after school for help in her classes. She is getting better grades now.

____

Sam does not like school and is planning to drop out. He doesn't do homework and is absent a lot.

____

Tony studies every day and tries to do extra-credit work whenever possible.

____

3. honesty

Louis will tell you exactly what he thinks about anything

____

Malisa will say just about anything to get what she wants.

____

Carla didn't want to hurt Ann's feelings, so she lied to her about what the other students said about her.

____

Name____ Date ______________

What Is Important to You?

Worksheet #6

Directions: Read the list of items below of things that you might value. Put a check mark next to those things that apply to you. Feel free to add items to the list.

Objects or Possessions

_____ a pet

_____ a trophy or ribbon

_____ a diploma

_____ favorite jeans or sweater

_____ computer

_____ video game

People

_____ sister, brother

_____ parent

_____ best friend

_____ teacher

_____ coach

_____ athlete

_____ celebrity

Personality Characteristic

_____ honesty

_____ good athlete

_____ sense of humor

_____ kind to others

_____ leader

_____ popular

_____ good-looking

Preferences

_____ having space to oneself

_____ peace and quiet

_____ being part of a group

_____ having someone to talk to

_____ having a car or way to get around independently

Lesson 3: Standards of Measurement

Placing value on something implies that there is some sort of measurement factor. How is it determined that something is of greater/lesser value than something else? Whether we actually are aware of it or not, we use standards or scales to evaluate and rate things that we value.

Objectives

- The student will identify several scales or standards of measurement that can be quantified.
- The student will give an example of a standard of measurement that does not involve numbers.

Introduction

Write ten simple but varied math problems on the board. Ask students to solve the problems and hand in their papers. Then inform them that the grade they get will not be based upon the number of correct answers, but how they formed the number "8." If they made two small circles, they will get an A on the assignment. If they formed the number any other way, they will get an F. Have students discuss the following questions:

- Why isn't this a fair way to judge their work?
- Would this be fair if the students were informed ahead of time that this was the standard of measurement?
- Why is it important for the standard of measurement to match the job? Isn't it silly for students to be rated for a math assignment on a completely different skill?

Worksheet #7: Standards of Measurement with Numbers

Synopsis: The fastest, tallest, shortest, smartest of something can be determined by competition, measurement, or setting up a test. In each of these examples, the rating can be performed by the use of numbers (height, speed, number of correct answers, etc.). Many times measurement is completed using a numerical system.

Directions: Have students determine a standard of measurement for each of the items on the worksheet.

Answers (examples):

1. time the horses with a stopwatch; 2. measure the height of the girls in the class; 3. look at the recipe to determine the quantity of sugar; 4. take a class vote on who is the most popular person; 5. examine the teacher's grading scale for what factors are important in this assignment (use of colors, demonstration of what was taught in class, etc.); 6. examine the teacher's grading scale for what factors are important in this assignment (capitalization, punctuation, typed neatly, outline given on time, etc.); 7. the number of people who have been to see the movie or the amount of money it has brought in; 8. how many tricks the dog knows; 9. look at the volume dial; 10. check his blood pressure, cholesterol level, weight, etc.

Discussion:

1. Why is it helpful to use numbers to rate something's value? (*makes it easier to quantify, put in order*)
2. What are some things that are harder to put numbers onto? (*the painting, for example, is subject to opinion*)
3. Could there be more than one way to measure something; for example, the smartest dog? (*yes, one person might record the number of tricks, another might record how quickly the dog obeyed, someone else might consider the smartest dog the one that learns a new trick the quickest, etc.*)

Worksheet #8: Putting Value on Something Without Numbers

Synopsis: Some things that are valued do not have a number that indicates how much it is valued; rather, it is valued because of a memory, feeling, or personal taste.

Directions: Students are to think about the values listed on the worksheet and consider how differently each of the two individuals value them and why they might view the situation differently.

Answers (examples):

1. The first person rates the painting based on technical qualities of the painting; the second person rates it on how the painting makes her feel.
2. The first person rates Kim Li as a very kind person based on what he has heard about her; the second bases his opinion of Kim Li on his experience with her.
3. The first person rates Michael Jordan as a great basketball player based on his abilities; the second does not consider him to be that great because that person does not value sports very much.

Discussion:

1. What are some other things people value that are very subjective or just a matter of opinion? (*a good restaurant, a good television show, a good politician*)
2. Do you think it is important to be able to give reasons to back up your opinion or is it OK just to have an opinion based on feeling alone?
3. Why is it important for a teacher to have a standard of measurement for grading you rather than grading your work depending on how he or she feels that day? (*feelings change; your grade should be the same if it is based on a consistent standard of measurement*)

Lesson Review

1. What are some things that can be evaluated or rated using numbers?
2. What are some things that cannot be evaluated or rated using numbers?

Journal-Entry Ideas

- Rate three friends of yours according to how good a friend he or she is. What scale are you using?
- What subjects in school are easy to grade or measure using numbers? Why? Which are not? Why?

Teacher Journal

Think about your "good" students, your "average" students, and your "poor" students. What rating scale are you using to categorize these students? Is it more than a percentage in your grade book? What other factors do you use on your rating scale to evaluate these students?

Goal for the Day

Today I give myself a grade on a scale of 1 to 10 (with 10 the highest) according to how well I:

- listened to my students
- used my sense of humor
- demonstrated patience
- got through all of my lesson plans
- dealt with that one difficult student

Name____ Date ______________

Standards of Measurement With Numbers

Worksheet #7

Directions: What standard of measurement might be used to assess the value of the following items?

1. fastest horse in a race:

   ____

2. tallest girl in the class:

   ____

3. how much sugar is in a batch of chocolate chip cookies:

   ____

4. how popular someone is:

   ____

5. what grade a painting would get in art class:

   ____

6. what grade a written report would get in English class:

   ____

7. how popular a movie is:

   ____

8. the smartest dog:

   ____

9. how loud the stereo is:

   ____

10. how healthy someone is:

    ____

    ____

Name____ Date ____________

Putting Value on Something Without Numbers

Worksheet #8

Directions: What standard of measurement is each student below using to show how he or she values or feels about each item or situation?

---

1. **Valuing a Work of Art**

---

2. **Valuing a Person**

---

3. **Valuing a Talent**

Lesson 4: Ups and Downs of Self-Esteem

Someone might feel that he or she is an excellent student, but is a loser when it comes to being attractive to the opposite sex. A pimple or a "bad hair day" might be enough to destroy one's self-confidence when it comes time to give an oral report. Self-esteem can be a fluctuating, conditional state of mind.

Objectives

- The student will rate relative levels of self-esteem in several different areas (e.g., intelligence, sociability) for a given individual.
- The student will compare two ratings of the same area for a given individual.

Introduction

Choose two students to act out the cartoon (or reproduce the cartoon for the class) at the end of this lesson. Ask students to consider how and why the perceptions of the first character are so different.

Worksheet #9: Rating Self-Esteem in Different Areas

Synopsis: Two fictitious students (one male, one female) give comments about their looks, intelligence, and sociability. In each case, the students' ratings differ for the three areas.

Directions: Students are to rate Mabu and Trina according to the comments each makes about himself or herself using the scale "high, medium, and low."

Answers (examples):

1. Mabu: looks – high, intelligence – medium, sociability – high
2. Trina: looks – low, intelligence – high, sociability – low

Discussion Questions:

1. What overall rating would you give Mabu and Trina for self-esteem?
2. Why is it difficult to give an "overall" rating? (*so many different components*)
3. Do you think if Trina felt differently about her looks, her rating would change in the other areas too? (*possibly*)
4. Do you think a change in one area of self-esteem can affect other areas? (*yes!*)

Worksheet #10: How Others Might Rate Self-Esteem in Different Areas

Synopsis: The fictitious students of Worksheet #9 are now rated (by fictitious individuals) and give another perspective of the student.

Directions: Students are to read the descriptions of the students from Worksheet #9 that are now described by a teacher and a peer. They are to complete a rating scale based on this new information.

Answers (examples):

1. Mabu: looks – high, intelligence – medium, sociability – high
2. Trina: looks – medium, intelligence – low, sociability – low

Discussion:

1. In what areas do Mabu and his science teacher seem to agree? (*in all areas*)
2. In what areas do Trina and her friend seem to agree? (*sociability*)
3. Why do you think the ratings are different in some ways? (*different perspective; the individual might not be accurate in his or her own perception of self*)

Lesson Review

1. Why wouldn't an individual have high or low self-esteem in all areas?
2. When rating self-esteem, how could it be helpful to have information about an individual from someone who knows the person?

Journal-Entry Ideas

- Write a paragraph describing the way you dress, comb your hair, or organize your locker. Write a second paragraph describing how you think a good friend of yours would complete this description of you. Then write a third paragraph as if your teacher, parent, or other adult were describing you.
- A good friend can set you straight about your abilities. Write about a time when you felt badly about something, felt as though you had failed, or were disappointed. How did a friend help you out?

Teacher Journal

When you're at lunch or in the teacher's lounge, what differing comments do you hear from others about a particular student? Is the student who is the object of discussion always in trouble? A problem in class? Do you hear more than one opinion expressed about him or her? Is the reputation slanted? Is it deserved? What comments do you make to enhance or change the tone of the conversation?

Goal for the Day

Today when I hear a student make a negative comment about something he or she has done, I will try to objectively turn it around—perhaps by questioning the student ("Why do you feel that way?") or adding my own perception ("You could have changed this, but you did a good job on that.").

I got a C on my report because I didn't follow the directions. I'm really stupid.
No, Tracy — you're not "stupid"; you just follow your own creative path! You're a thinker!

It's Friday night and once again, I don't have a date. I'm pathetically unpopular.
You're not "unpopular"; you are independent! You don't need to be socially restrained by other people!

I was afraid to step on the scale because I thought I'd break it. I am so FAT!
"Fat?" Ha! You're a substantial person, unafraid of that second dessert! You're bold!

I can't keep even a part-time job. I'm such a loser.
You're not a "loser"; you're a thrill-seeker! You need constant excitement!

My dad keeps telling me I'm lazy because my room is a mess.
Oh, no, — you're not "lazy"; you just work at your own pace and have your own unique system of organization.

I have no friends because I'm self-centered, depressed, and I make everyone around me feel miserable.

Why are you so quiet?
I'm not being "quiet"; I'm totally agreeing with your very accurate analysis!

Name____ Date ______________

Rating Self-Esteem in Different Areas

Worksheet #

Directions: Below is an imaginary rating scale of several individuals for three categories: look intelligence, and sociability. After reading each person's description, fill out the rating scale according how you think they would rate themselves. Use check marks.

1. **Mabu:** I think I am a rather good-looking guy. I'm tall, have dark hair, and most people think have a nice smile. I wish I did a little better in school, however. My grades are not the greates but I think that's because I have a very active social life. I can't wait for the weekends: party! part party! I like to get together with my friends and have a really good time.

	Looks	**Intelligence**	**Sociability**
high			
medium			
low			

2. **Trina:** I'm really good-looking if you like girls who are overweight and have impossible hair. N wonder I've never had a date — the only girls that guys around here will go out with are th cheerleaders, and everyone knows that they have no brains at all. I like school most of the tim but I don't have time to study because I have to work. My grades are passable, but I know I coul get straight A's if I really wanted to. Most of the kids around my school are real jerks. I've got on good friend, and we do a lot together. I don't care if a lot of people like me or not.

	Looks	**Intelligence**	**Sociability**
high			
medium			
low			

Name________________________________ Date ____________

How Others Might Rate Self-Esteem in Different Areas

Worksheet #10

Directions: Compare the following descriptions of Mabu and Trina with their self-reports (from Worksheet #9). Fill out the rating scales according to how someone else would rate Mabu and Trina. Use check marks.

1. **Mr. Goldstein, Mabu's Science Teacher**: Mabu is really Mr. Popularity around school. It must be nice to be so good-looking! As long as he has an audience, he's happy. Kids really seem to like him. And I must admit, teachers like him too. We often discuss his creative excuses in the teacher's lounge. I wish Mabu would study harder, because I know he could get good grades if he tried. He's a likeable guy, but he should do more with himself and his abilities.

	Looks	Intelligence	Sociability
high			
medium			
low			

2. **Amy, Trina's best friend:** Trina is always putting herself down. Sure, she's a little overweight but she makes it sound as though she's a blimp. I think she's really cute, especially when she takes the time to fix her hair. Neither one of us does well in school. Trina has always had trouble with math. She just can't seem to catch on. She's not part of the popular crowd, but then not many kids are at our school. We just hang around together and try not to get into trouble. One guy asked her out last semester, but she said she wasn't interested in dating anybody. I think she would have more friends if she would act interested in other people, but she keeps to herself. She works a lot of hours at her job, too. It takes a lot of time to make and keep friends.

	Looks	Intelligence	Sociability
high			
medium			
low			

Lesson 5: Rating Your Self-Esteem

At this point, students may only have a rudimentary idea of what self-esteem is. This lesson is simply a baseline for students to record their initial perceptions of themselves at this time. You may want to compare this rating with a similar rating that students can complete at the end of the workbook when they have more knowledge and insight into self-esteem.

Objective

- The student will complete a personal rating scale based on his or her feelings in several categories (looks, family, accomplishments, etc.).

Introduction

Display several pictures of faces of celebrities — perhaps a political figure, movie star, model, etc. Have students discuss in which areas of life they would rate the person "high" in self- esteem. Or, reverse the procedure and have students think of someone who they would suspect would rate him- or herself highly in looks, intelligence, bravery, sociability, etc.

Worksheet #11: Rating Your Self-Esteem

Synopsis: Students can begin thinking about their self-esteem by completing a rating scale on several categories.

Directions: Students are to consider the categories on the worksheet and rate themselves according to how they feel about themselves in that area. Rating scales could be 1-10, high/medium/low, or whatever rating scale is suitable for the student.

Discussion Questions:

1. Which of the categories on the worksheet do you think will change in your rating over the next few days? Why?
2. Which of the categories do you have much control over?
3. Which of the categories do you have little control over?
4. When you think of "accomplishments," do you think more in terms of what you have already accomplished or things that you are currently working on?
5. If you had to pool all of the categories together and come up with only one rating for your self-esteem, what would it be?

Lesson Review

1. What are some different areas or categories that affect your self-esteem?
2. In which areas would you rate your self-esteem high?
3. In which areas would you rate your self-esteem low?
4. How would you rate your overall self-esteem at this time?

Journal-Entry Ideas

- Think about a recent experience in which you were so angry, hurt, or bothered that you could hardly think of anything else. Describe this experience. How did it affect how you felt about yourself?
- Think about a recent experience in which you felt happy, wonderful, or excited about something. Describe this experience. How did it make you feel about yourself?

TEACHER JOURNAL

Getting a handle on your self-esteem is an important step toward helping your students do the same. List several categories that are important to you and jot down a few sentences describing how you feel about each.

GOAL FOR THE DAY

Today I will make positive comments about myself and my abilities in front of my students. I can be a good model for them and, at the same time, reinforce my strengths out loud to myself!

Name________________________________ Date ____________

Rating Your Self-Esteem

Worksheet #

Directions: Realizing that self-esteem changes constantly, rate your feelings about yourself for th following categories as you view them today. You might want to add some comments that explain wh you rated yourself as you did.

How I feel about my . . .

1. looks ______________________________

____

____

2. success in school ______________________________

____

____

3. intelligence ______________________________

____

____

4. physical abilities or talents ______________________________

____

____

5. friends ______________________________

____

____

6. family ______________________________

____

____

7. accomplishments ______________________________

____

____

8. self as a person ______________________________

____

____

____

Lesson 6: The Importance of High Self-Esteem

Who cares if you have high self-esteem or not? People who have high self-esteem are not only better equipped to handle whatever life deals them, but they also can contribute to making a better life for themselves and others.

Objectives

- The student will match examples of individuals with high self-esteem with a reason why high self-esteem is important.
- The student will give examples of how having high self-esteem can empower an individual in life situations.

Introduction

Ask students to give you reasons why they think having a good or high self-esteem is important. List the reasons on the board or on a sheet that you can save and display.

WORKSHEET #12: THE IMPORTANCE OF HIGH SELF-ESTEEM

Synopsis: There are many benefits to having high self-esteem, including personal empowerment, outlook on life, and making changes for one's self and others.

Directions: Students are to match the individual on the left side of the worksheet who is giving a comment about a situation with the reason why a high self-esteem is important on the right side of the worksheet. Students can put the letter of the reason on the line next to the example.

Answers:

1. F; 2. B; 3. A; 4. E; 5. D; 6. C

Discussion Questions:

1. How do you think each of the individuals would have handled or commented on their situations if they had low self-esteem?
2. Do you think the individuals on the worksheet might have made the comments out loud or just thought them to themselves? Would it make a difference in the outcome?

WORKSHEET #13: THE POWER OF HIGH SELF-ESTEEM

Synopsis: There are many applications of having high self-esteem. Students can find and state applications in their own experience.

Directions: On the worksheet, several reasons why having high self-esteem is important are stated. Students are to think of personal situations or examples of how these reasons apply in their own experience.

Answers (examples):

1. getting your parents to change your curfew by giving a logical argument stating your good behavior; 2. realizing that a bad grade on one test is simply that: one test; 3. trying out for a new sport even though you probably won't make the team; 4. being able to be supportive of a sibling who is going through family problems; 5. you can listen to comments from a boss or teacher without crying and feeling awful; 6. you know that when it's your turn at bat, you will do a decent job!

LESSON REVIEW

1. What are some reasons why having a high self-esteem is important?
2. Give an example from your own experience of someone demonstrating a high self-esteem in a problem situation.

Journal-Entry Ideas

- What was the last risk you took? What made you finally decide to go for it? How did you feel after you tried it? Did you have any regrets?
- What one change would you like to see happen in your life? What could you do to work towards making that change happen?
- Think about a time when you were disappointed, devastated, or ready to give up. What comments did you make out loud or to yourself? Now rewrite that scene . . . and this time write it as though you have incredibly high self-esteem. What comments would you make this time?

Teacher Journal

Think about the last time you directly caused something to change for the better. What did you do, what did you say, how did you cause it to happen? How did you feel after you sat back and looked at what you did?

Goal for the Day

Today I will walk around, doing my job, but with an awareness of the power within me that comes from my strong self-esteem. Instead of reacting negatively to whatever comes my way, I will take a second to mentally conjure up my protective shield of a healthy self-esteem and deflect any harsh comments, feelings of making a mistake, or undeserved criticism.

Name________________________________ Date ____________

Importance of High Self-Esteem

Worksheet #12

Directions: The individuals below are examples of people with high self-esteem. Match the individual on the left with the reason why high self-esteem is important on the right. Write the letter of the reason next to the person.

1. It doesn't matter that Frank said I wasn't doing a good job. I know that my work is good.

   ____

2. I'm really disappointed that I didn't get the scholarship, but I'll find another way to pay for college.

   ____

3. This policy is not right. I think I can organize people to help get things changed.

   ____

4. Marie said some mean things to me, but I know she's having a bad day. I'm not going to let it affect me. I'll talk to her about it later.

   ____

5. I wish my parents weren't getting a divorce, but I know it's not my fault. We'll survive.

   ____

6. This project seems really hard. I don't know if I can do it, but I'm going to give it a try. If I fail . . . I'll just try again.

   ____

A. High self-esteem affects your ability to make needed changes.

B. High self-esteem makes it possible to handle life's disappointments.

C. High self-esteem gives you confidence to take risks.

D. High self-esteem lets you realize that you are not responsible for every bad or unpleasant thing that happens to you.

E. High self-esteem lets you handle unfair criticism or comments from others without falling apart.

F. High self-esteem allows you to believe in your worth, even if others try to make you doubt it.

Name________________________________ Date ____________

The Power of High Self-Esteem

Worksheet #1

Directions: Below are some reasons why having high self-esteem is important. For each reason give an example of how someone could draw on the power of high self-esteem to overcome a problem or to make something better.

Reason 1: You can make changes!

____

____

____

Reason 2: You can handle disappointments!

____

____

____

Reason 3: You can take risks with confidence in yourself!

____

____

____

Reason 4: You realize that you are not always at fault for every bad or unpleasant thing that happens!

____

____

____

Reason 5: You can handle criticism from others!

____

____

____

Reason 6: You believe in yourself!

____

____

____

Lesson 7: A Model for Thinking About Self-Esteem

It is often helpful to use a "model" for picturing new ideas. In this lesson, students compare a healthy body with a healthy self-esteem.

Objectives

- The student will identify ways in which a human body becomes strong, remains healthy, and adapts to new situations.
- The student will compare specific ways in which developing a healthy self-esteem is similar to ways in which a human body develops in a healthy manner.

Introduction

Ask students to give you a list of five things their parents told them to do (or perhaps still remind them to do!) to stay healthy as they were growing up. (*e.g., eat everything on your plate, don't read in the dark, don't swim right after eating, etc.*)

Worksheet #14: A Model for Self-Esteem

Synopsis: A healthy self-esteem can be compared in several ways to a healthy body. Both begin with potential, grow and change over time, adapt to new situations, and require care.

Directions: Students are to complete the outline of ways in which a healthy body is similar to a healthy self-esteem. From the list of Healthy Body Ideas, students are to write the letter of the example (a-f) in each of the six categories. Then, using examples from the list of Healthy Self-Esteem Ideas, students are to write the letter of those examples (g-l) next to those of the Healthy Body. You may want to do the first item in each list together with students as an example of how to complete the worksheet.

Answers:

Healthy Body – 1. d; 2. c; 3. a; 4. e; 5. b; 6. f

Healthy Self-Esteem – 1. h; 2. k; 3. j; 4. l; 5. g; 6. i

Discussion Questions:

1. Some people are not born with healthy bodies. What are some examples? (*vision problems, asthma, deformities, etc.*)
2. How do people overcome some of those handicapping conditions? (*learn to work around situations, use medication, therapy*)
3. How do some people overcome poor self-esteem conditions? (*learn to use strengths, listen to people who can help them, develop new skills, etc.*)
4. What are some ways to keep your body healthy? (*exercise, eat right*)
5. What are some ways to keep your self-esteem healthy? (*take risks, know yourself, develop friendships, etc.*)

Lesson Review

1. How is a healthy body similar to a healthy self-esteem? Give at least three ways they are similar.
2. Give a specific example for each of your three ways in #1 so you could keep your body healthy and your self-esteem healthy.

Journal-Entry Ideas

- What are some ways you take care of your body? Do you feel that this is important?
- What is one way you could work on keeping your self-esteem healthy? Be specific about what you could do.

Teacher Journal

Is there a connection between physical and mental fitness? Think of one thing you do for yourself to keep your body healthy. Can you go one step further and add something you know you should be doing to keep yourself healthy?

Goal for the Day

Make a poster of the completed model comparing a healthy body and healthy self-esteem. Place it somewhere in the room where you and students can view it easily and often. Throughout the day (or week) identify moments in which you are growing, exercising, learning, developing, or taking care of yourself — your body or your self-esteem.

Name________________________________ Date ______________

A Model for Self-Esteem

Worksheet # 14

Directions: A model can be helpful to compare something you are learning about with something you are already familiar. Study the following comparison of a healthy body and a healthy self-esteem. Then fill in the outline with examples from the lists below.

	Healthy Body	Healthy Self-Esteem
1. Know that you are born with certain potential or resources.	________	________
2. You grow and change with time and experience.	________	________
3. Exercise or use your abilities to improve yourself and stay strong.	________	________
4. Learn about yourself; create an awareness of how your body/self works.	________	________
5. Develop and use support systems that are around you.	________	________
6. Take care of yourself.	________	________

Healthy Body Ideas

a. Jog regularly or work out to stay fit.

b. Visit your doctor or other health care professional when necessary; read articles about good health.

c. Get taller; become stronger; speak, think, and use your muscles to get where you want to go.

d. You have ten fingers, a well-developed heart, vision, and good lungs.

e. Learn to warm up before exercising; don't eat certain foods that will give you a stomach-ache later; know what you may be allergic to.

f. Join a health club; walk around the park with friends; visit your eye doctor yearly; eat right; don't smoke.

Healthy Self-Esteem

g. Develop friendships and relationships with others; know who you can trust; join a support group if you need to.

h. You have an awareness that you are a person; you have a mind and a body and can use them both.

i. Stay out of trouble; think positively about yourself; put yourself in good situations.

j. Take risks; develop new skills; learn new things.

k. Learn to relate to other people; listen to what they say; form ideas about yourself as you grow and interact with others.

l. Understand what things make you angry and react badly; know who you should avoid; figure out how to reward yourself.

Lesson 8: A Few Basic Beliefs

The "bottom line" to thinking about self-esteem is simply that people have worth. Without this premise, there is no basis for anything that follows about developing self-esteem. In this lesson, students are introduced to several basic ideas that are the foundation for everything else that follows.

Objectives

- The student will explain or summarize the four basic beliefs about self-esteem as presented in the lesson.
- The student will give an example of how each of the four basic beliefs can be substantiated.

Introduction

1. Write the following controversial statements on the board:
   - People should be allowed to commit suicide if they want to.
   - Convicted murderers should be put to death.
   - Everyone is a wonderful person.
   - People with handicaps can't contribute anything to the world.
2. Have students respond to the statements. It will be hard to be nonjudgmental, but allow students to voice their opinions. There will probably be a lively discussion if you have some vocal students with strong opinions.
3. Close the introductory period by concluding that people do not always agree with certain positions and certainly do have different opinions about things. Although we are entitled to having our own opinions, hopefully those opinions are formed not only by feelings, but by attention to facts, exposure to life situations, and adhering to a moral code that we can honestly live with. Inform students that a lot of the lessons that follow will be based on a few basic beliefs — and even if the students disagree with those beliefs (and some may), challenge them to understand the position and statements even if they do not at this point agree with them.

Worksheet #15: A Few Basic Beliefs

Synopsis: Four basic beliefs are presented that are the foundation for the rest of the book. Hopefully, students will agree with the premises, but if not, at least they can agree to try to understand the premises.

Directions: Students are to indicate whether they agree or disagree with the four premises on the worksheet. They can put a check mark in the box to indicate they agree. Students can also add their own examples to substantiate their opinions.

Discussion Questions:

1. What people do you feel do not have any worth, if you did not agree with statement #1? (*handicapped people, old people, evil people, etc.*)
2. Do you think most people are capable of learning? achieving? making others happy? doing something right? Even if they do not choose to exercise this option?
3. Do you think sick people can ever become well? Evil people can ever become good? People with bad attitudes can ever change?
4. How do you think people learn to recognize that they are valuable? (*they learn about success, they listen to what others say about them*)
5. If someone does not believe he or she is valuable, does it matter that you do? (*you may be the change agent!*)

6. How do people show they value other people, even people whom they do not know? (*are polite to others; give money to charities; etc.*)

Worksheet #16: I'm Worth It!

Synopsis: After being somewhat familiar with the four premises in Worksheet #15, students are given examples of comments that illustrate the premises.

Directions: Students are to match the four basic premises at the top of the worksheet with the comments of individuals that follow. In all but one example, the comments are positive examples of the premise.

Answers:

4, 2, 3, 1

Discussion Questions:

1. Everyone has worth. How does the pastor visiting the prisoners on death row illustrate that belief?
2. What changes could someone on death row make that would matter to anyone? (*apologize to victim or family of victim; make restitution; affect those around them in a positive way; make moral decisions*)
3. A person can learn to recognize that he or she is a valuable person. What did Sharon need to learn? (*that she was an innocent victim in the situation*)
4. How did Sharon learn this? (*through counseling, etc.*)
5. A person must believe he or she is a valuable person. Why doesn't Pietro believe this? (*he thinks he is stupid because he cannot read*)
6. Will anything ever change with Pietro until he believes in himself? (*hard to say — attitude is pretty important with learning, especially when learning is difficult; if he continues to resist, nothing may change*)
7. A high self-esteem gives you strength, etc. What challenges did Otis take on? (*poor background, financial situation, etc.*)
8. What makes you suspect that Otis has high self-esteem? (*comment: "I knew I could do it"*)

Lesson Review

1. What are four basic beliefs about self-esteem?
2. Give an example of an individual who believes and demonstrates each of the four basic beliefs.

Journal-Entry Ideas

- Do you really believe everyone has worth? What individuals or groups of people do you have difficulty with?
- Do you believe you are a valuable person? To whom are you valuable? What makes you valuable?
- Do you believe everyone is capable of changing — whether it is changing an attitude, a physical situation, or a social setting? What are some things you don't think can ever change for people?

Teacher Journal

Write down the four basic beliefs. After each, write the name of a student who is a good example of each. Then, think again, and write down the name of a student who is not a likely candidate to make that statement. To which student do you find most difficulty attributing worth? Which is most likely to resist recognizing value in himself or herself?

Goal for the Day

Make a statement verifying his or her worth to each of the students you listed above — the four who are easy to praise and the four who will make you work a little harder.

Name____________________ Date __________

A Few Basic Beliefs

Worksheet #15

Directions: Below are some premises, or basic beliefs, about self esteem. Put a check mark in the box if you agree with the statement. Add your own ideas or examples.

☐ 1. Everyone has worth.

☐ 2. A person can learn to recognize that he or she is a valuable person.

☐ 3. A person must believe he or she is a valuable person.

☐ 4. A high self-esteem gives you strength to be happy with yourself, make changes, take on challenges, and appreciate life.

Name________________________________ Date ______________

I'm Worth It!

Worksheet #16

Directions: Match the basic beliefs listed below with the comments that follow. Which basic belie is illustrated by the speaker's statements? Write the number of the basic belief next to the comments.

1. Everyone has worth.
2. A person can learn to recognize that he or she is a valuable person.
3. A person must believe he or she is a valuable person.
4. A high self-esteem gives you strength to be happy with yourself, make changes, take on challenges and appreciate life.

_______ Otis was the first child in his family to finish high school, go to college, and eventually become a lawyer. No one would have thought that because of his poverty-stricken background, minority status, and dangerous neighborhood, Otis would ever amount to anything. "I knew I could do it," Otis commented when questioned about his success. "I wanted to get out of that life, and I did." Now he counsels and represents young people from the streets who do not see a way out of a dismal life.

_______ Sharon had been abused by her grandfather from the time she was eleven years old. She went through many years of school feeling as though she was worthless, dirty, and unimportant. It was not until several years later, after lots of counseling with school and legal agencies, that she realized it was not her fault and that she was capable of being a strong individual.

_______ No matter how many times teachers, relatives, and counselors told Pietro that he was a good person, Pietro refused to believe that he was important in any respect because he was in middle school and still could not read. "How can I not be stupid?" he asks. "I can't even read."

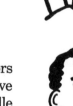

_______ A pastor visits the prisoners on death row at a state prison every week. He doesn't care what they have done; he doesn't even ask. He continues to tell the prisoners that they are valuable people and their lives are not over. Even in prison, they can change themselves and affect others.

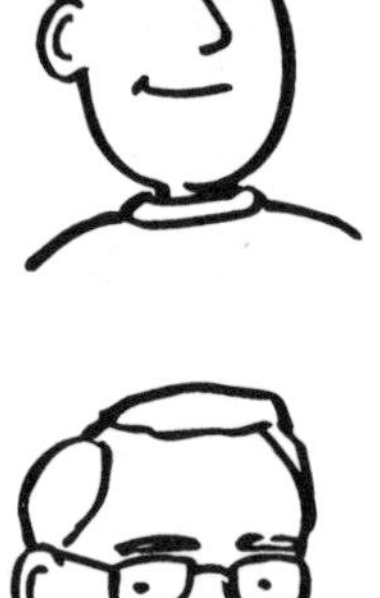

Part II

Factors That Affect Self-Esteem

Nine lessons and twenty-one worksheets cover the factors that can affect how an individual develops his or her self-esteem. Family members, peer groups, life experiences, and individual talents and abilities are just a few of the topics that your students will encounter in this very extensive section.

Lesson 9: Family Factors

The development of an individual's self-esteem begins at birth. The family into which he or she is born can affect how the individual begins to view himself or herself. Was he a wanted child? Is she a middle child? Is the family dealing with economic problems? Are the mother and father limited in their parenting skills? Is the father present in the home? There are many influences from the family upon the child as soon as he or she is born.

Objectives

- The student will determine whether a given comment is the result of someone's behavior or someone's comment about the person.
- The student will summarize a given comment in terms of how it would make a child feel.
- The student will recognize reactions of individuals in family situations that reflect a strong or healthy self-esteem.

Introduction

Make a chart on the board that tallies the numbers of students who are the oldest, middle, or youngest children in the family. Ask students if they like their position in the family and allow a few minutes for them to discuss the relative benefits and drawbacks to their family order.

Worksheet #17: What Others Say and Do

Synopsis: From the time we become family members, we learn about ourselves (and subsequently our self-esteem) by paying attention to how we are treated by others. Two ways in which a family can influence a child are by what they tell a child and how they behave around the child.

Directions: Students are to read the comments in the middle of the worksheet that are statements from an individual. They are then to draw a line to the side of the worksheet that indicates the comment is an example of how another person treats the individual or an example of what another person says to the individual.

Answers: 1. says; 2. treated; 3. treated; 4. says; 5. treated; 6. treated

Discussion Questions:

1. Which is more important in affecting someone's self-esteem: how others talk to them or how they are treated? Does it make any difference? (*probably not; depends on the individual*)
2. Why do you think what children hear from their parents is so important, especially at a young age? (*young children tend to believe what they hear, especially from their parents*)
3. In which of the examples is a family member trying to promote good self-esteem in the individual? (*only #6*)

Worksheet #18: Family Situations

Synopsis: Examples are given of what parents say to their children. These messages may help or hurt the child's self-esteem, depending on what the child hears from the message.

Directions: Students are to read the comments and then decide what message the child would actually hear or determine from each comment. Students can either answer orally or rewrite the comment in a simpler form.

Answers: (examples):

1. I was a burden to you. 2. You don't want to spend time with me. 3. I was really wanted! 4. My parents' needs are more important than mine. 5. I am the cause of your disappointment in life. 6. You are happy to see parts of yourself in me. 7. School is not very important. 8. It is important to make time for our family to spend together.

Discussion Questions:

1. Do you think the parents on this worksheet intended to make their child feel particularly good or bad? Which ones? *(some parents probably don't think about what their message is to their children)*
2. Do you think a bad day or a time of stress would cause a parent to say something hurtful to a child? *(yes)*
3. How do you think it would make a child feel to believe that he or she was not even wanted before birth? *(pretty lousy)*
4. Children do not ask to be born; it is not anything they can control. How would this affect someone who felt that he or she was unwanted? *(accept that they do not have to take the responsibility for being born or causing trouble; it had nothing to do with them or their decision!)*

WORKSHEET #19: THOUGHTS ABOUT YOUR FAMILY

Synopsis: This is a personal experience for the student and you should not expect every student to share his or her family problems. But it allows students to reflect upon what other family members say to them and how they are treated and then to relate these feelings to their self-esteem.

Directions: Students are to list the members of their family. This could be the people with whom they live, family members whom they see regularly, or individuals whom they consider to be family. The students are to think of examples of ways that these individuals affect their self-esteem, in both positive and negative ways.

Discussion Questions:

Note: Students can volunteer information about their families if appropriate. The purpose is not to pry into family problems, but rather to discuss and think about ways that family members can help each other (even if it is by using a negative example).

1. Most kids have problems at some time or another with their parents. In general, what types of problems come up? *(authority; nagging parents; unfair rules; curfew problems; school situations; etc.)*
2. What are some ways you can think of in which parents can help support their children and help their self-esteem? *(go to sports events; check homework; ask about how they're doing; etc.)*
3. Again, most people have trouble getting along with brothers and sisters at times. What do you think are some common sources of these problems? *(sharing a room; having stepsisters and -brothers; unequal treatment; etc.)*
4. How could an older brother or sister be a positive support for someone? *(help with homework; look out for them if someone is bullying them; show them how to throw a baseball; etc.)*

WORKSHEET #20: FAMILY SUPPORT

Synopsis: On this worksheet, two examples of family problems are given. The student must select the response that better shows a healthy response to the problem.

Directions: The student is to read the situations on the worksheet that involve an individual having to make a decision about a family situation. The student is to select the response that demonstrates a healthy self-esteem.

Answers: 1. a; 2. b

Discussion:

1. Why do you think Maria's parents are so suspicious of what she does? *(very protective, don't trust her, don't trust her friends)*
2. If Maria were the kind of person who didn't believe in herself, how might she respond? *(like answer b; retaliate by threatening them)*
3. How does Maria's response show that her self-esteem is strong? *(she can accept another point of view; she understands that her parents have fears; she is not threatened by what they are doing; she is able to take positive steps to include them with the hopes that they will make changes too)*
4. What kind of relationship does Alex have with his sister? *(pretty good – they share things)*
5. Even though Alex needs the money, why does he consider Kesna a good risk to pay back the money? *(she is looking for a job; college is a temporary situation; she has paid back money before)*
6. How does this show that Alex has a good self-esteem? *(he is not hoarding the money; he is able to trust another person; he is confident that his own situation will be under control; he is not worried about terrible things happening; he believes in his sister and the worth of what she is doing)*

Lesson Review

1. What are two ways in which a child learns about his or her self-esteem from family members?
2. Give an example of a positive statement that a parent or other family member could make to improve a child's self-esteem.
3. Give an example of a positive behavior that a parent or other family member could do to improve a child's self-esteem.

Journal-Entry Ideas

- Think about your earliest childhood memories. What comes to mind? Were the experiences pleasant or unpleasant?
- When was the last argument you had with a family member? What was it about? How was it resolved? Now that it's over, do you feel it was a big deal?
- When you become a parent, how will you treat your children differently from the way your parents treated you?
- What is the nicest, most important comment that you have ever heard a parent say about you? How did it make you feel?
- Has there ever been a time of crisis in your family when everyone had to pull together to help each other? What happened? What happened to the family during the crisis and when it was all over?

Teacher Journal

In what ways are you like your parents? Are you a teacher because somehow one or both of them influenced you to go into teaching? You are their legacy. What did they give you?

Goal for the Day

I may be the closest thing to a parent or a family member to some of my students. Today I will think of myself not just as a teacher, a paid professional who is here to educate a mind, but as a human being who may need to listen, to nurture, to be a good example of a caring adult for my students.

Name____ Date ______________

What Others Say and Do

Worksheet #17

Directions: Draw a line from the statement in the middle towards the left if it is an example of how someone is treated; draw a line towards the right if it is an example of what someone says.

How a Person Is Treated		**What Someone Says About a Person**

1. No matter how good my grades are, my parents tell me that I should be doing better.

2. When I walk into the room, my mother and father stop talking. It makes me feel like they don't want me to know what's going on.

3. It doesn't seem to matter that I got to the TV first and am really interested in watching my favorite show; my older brother just walks in front of me and changes the channel to whatever he wants without even asking.

4. My aunt tells me that I would look a lot better if I would only lose 10 pounds, get contacts, and dye my hair.

5. I tried to talk to my grandfather about the problems I'm having at school, but he doesn't seem to listen to me.

6. My dad spends time with me every evening after he gets home from work on my free-throw shooting. I want to make the team, but I know I need extra practice.

Name______________________________ Date ______________

Family Situations

Worksheet #18

Directions: What message do the following statements from parents give to a child?

1. "Five children are too many. When you were born, we were already deep in debt from the other four."

   ____

2. "Your mother and I don't have time to take you on a field trip this weekend, but here is some money. I'm sure you'll find something fun to do."

   ____

3. "We wanted a child for ten years before you born. I don't think we ever wanted anything more than a child."

   ____

4. "There is never any money around here. Don't even ask for new clothes, because we can't afford them. However, I'm planning to go out drinking after work with the people I work with. I won't be back until quite late."

   ____

5. "I got pregnant in high school. The father disappeared and I ended up dropping out of school to get a job. I'll never have the chance to be successful because I had to give up everything for you."

   ____

6. "When I look at you, I see the best parts of your mother and father. I think about all of the wonderful things that are going to happen to you in your life."

   ____

7. "I know I should make you get up early and go to school, but I'm so tired. If you miss school occasionally, I guess that'll be the way it is. Unless of course you can get up by yourself and make it to school. There's probably some cereal around here somewhere."

   ____

8. "Wednesday nights are reserved for our family to do something together. No friends come over, no phone calls are made — we just spend time with the children doing something we all enjoy."

   ____

Name____ Date ____________

Thoughts About Your Family

Worksheet #19

Directions: List the members of your immediate family (examples: mother, father, sister, brother, grandparents, uncle, aunt, cousin, stepfather, stepmother). What are some ways they affect your self-esteem by how you are treated or what they say about you or to you? Put a + or - next to each example to indicate how it affects you.

Name____ Date ______________

Family Support

Worksheet #20

Directions: Read the following situations and the reactions of a person to each situation. Put an X in front of the reaction that shows a healthy self-esteem.

1. Maria's parents are very suspicious of everything she does. She feels she can't even go out on her own without them questioning where she has been, who she has been with, and what she has been doing. Maria is getting very tired of having to report her activities, especially when she is not doing anything wrong.

_____ a. Maria realizes her parents are protective of her and want to know what she is doing. She tries to include them in some of her activities and talks to them about what's going on at school, what she's thinking about, and other things on her mind. Maybe her parents are afraid she will get into trouble. Maybe they are sorry to see her grow up and lose her dependence on them.

_____ b. Maria has decided that her parents are too nosey and need to give her some space. She gives them a threat: either they start leaving her alone or she will find someplace else to live.

2. Alex has been saving money for months by doing odd jobs. He hopes to have enough to buy himself a motorcycle, since he can't afford a car. His older sister, Kesna, is in college and doesn't have enough money to buy books for the second semester. She asked him for a loan — the money he had been saving for a motorcycle. She has always paid back her loans and is looking for a part-time job.

_____ a. Alex decides that his sister needs to be more conscientious about saving money and that it would be a good lesson for her to learn to get a second job and earn the money on her own.

_____ b. Alex wants to help his sister, so he gives her enough of his money to get the books. He believes that she will repay him and maybe at some point he will need something from her. It might delay his getting the motorcycle, but he feels that his sister really needs to get through college right now. His turn might come later.

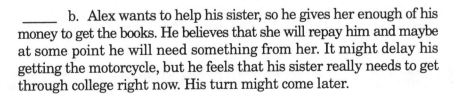

Lesson 10: Relationships with Friends

We choose our friends. Friendship is a special kind of relationship in which needs are expressed and met with reciprocity. When I need help, I look for you. When you need help, I'm there. However, as with most other relationships, friendships change over time, through events, and as people change. Yet the ability to form friendships and use (not abuse) what others can offer is something that is important to our self-esteem.

Objectives

- The student will identify examples of how individuals have demonstrated a positive influence on others.
- The student will identify examples in which individuals have demonstrated behaviors that are not conducive to building up another's self-esteem.

Introduction

Ask students to think of a person whom they would consider to be a good friend. You might want them to list the name on a piece of paper (not to be revealed). Then have them list at least two reasons or ways in which that person has demonstrated good friendship towards him or her.

Worksheet #21: Good Friends

Synopsis: People often demonstrate good friendship skills in times of crisis, ordinary change, or through specific events. These skills can help another feel important, worthy of attention, and cared about.

Directions: Students are to read the examples on the worksheet of friends who have helped other friends. Then they are to identify (orally or in writing) how the friend's action helped the other person and particularly how it would affect his or her self-esteem.

Answers:

1. Sharon went out of her way to help the individual feel included. This would make her feel important and cared about; 2. Juan realized that the person felt bad about striking out. This took some of the pressure off of him and probably made him feel included as part of the team; 3. Kaneesha gave up her own agenda to spend time during the crisis with her friend. This gave the friend emotional support during a crucial time; 4. Mike spent time teaching the other boy how to work on a car. This would improve the boy's skills and make him feel important; 5. Angela was loyal to the girl. Even though the friendship was not currently active, it made the girl feel respected.

Discussion Questions:

1. What definition would you give for **friend?** *(someone who is loyal to you, shares interests, gives-and-takes, etc.)*
2. In what ways can a good solid friendship help someone's self-esteem? *(the examples on the worksheet–feeling important, feeling cared about, feeling respected, learning new skills, etc.)*
3. Why is it sometimes easier to talk to a friend about a problem rather than a parent, counselor, adult, or someone else? *(the friend knows you, maybe went through a similar experience, etc.)*

Worksheet #22: Could-Be-Better Friends

Synopsis: Unfortunately, not everyone who starts out as a friend continues with that status. Over time, friendships change and it is sadly true that some friends are not "true"; they can forget loyalty in a hurry.

Directions: Students are to read the comments by individuals on the worksheet that reflect negative or derogatory comments about another person who is supposed to be a friend. Students are to identify (orally or in writing) how these actions or comments would affect someone's self-esteem.

Answers:

1. The girl implies that the friend looks fine, but really thinks she looks funny. The friend might find out that she was talking about her or laughing at her behind her back. 2. This person appears to be lending his car, but really expects a great deal in return. This is not an offer of friendship; it is an obligation ("do my homework"???) that is not fair to the friend. 3. This person is not being supportive; in fact, it sounds as though he is blaming his friend for losing the game. 4. The girls are not including Tracy in a party. If Tracy finds out, she will feel left out. 5. This person has turned off Ann; she is probably jealous of Ann's job and has judged her already. Ann would probably be upset to find that this reputation is being passed around about her. 6. This boy expected his friend to cover for him in a lie, but when he didn't, the boy got upset and said that Robert was not a good friend. This would make Robert feel like he let the boy down, even though Robert probably was in the right!

Discussion Questions:

1. Do you want a friend to always tell you the truth, even when you think it might hurt you or hurt your feelings?
2. In the second example, the boy expected quite a return for lending his car. Do you think this is fair? Is it OK for friends to make deals with each? *(sometimes; sure, as long as the deal is fair)*
3. What could the boy in example #3 have said that would have made his friend feel better? *("Nice try"; "You'll get it next time"; "Want to do some extra practicing after school?")*
4. People often gossip about each other when someone is successful. Why do you think that is? *(makes them feel better to put someone else down)*
5. Should friends lie for each other? Under what conditions? *(if someone is in danger or could get into a lot of trouble by lying, the friend should take that into account)*
6. How do you know when it's time to get rid of a friend and find some better people to hang out with? *(when you find out that your friend is betraying you; when you lose interests in the same things; when the friendship is unequal–one takes all the time and doesn't give, etc.)*

Lesson Review

1. Give two examples of statements or behaviors that a friend could do to support someone's self-esteem.
2. Give two examples of statements or behaviors that a friend could do that are harmful to someone's self-esteem.

Journal-Entry Ideas

- Think about a time in which a friend really came through for you. What were the circumstances?
- Think about a time in which a friend let you down or betrayed you. How did you feel? What is your relationship like with this person now?
- What kind of a friend are you? How would other people characterize you as a friend?

Teacher Journal

As adults, we base our friendship on factors other than who will make us popular and who plays on the same team that we do. Many adults only need a few close friends, not a lot of people to form our support group. Who do you consider to be a close friend? What factors form the basis of this friendship? How does this friend encourage your self-esteem? What do you do to encourage your friend?

Goal for the Day

Today I will make a phone call, write a letter, or make contact in some way with a friend who means a lot to me. I will offer a listening ear, encouragement, or perhaps share a good joke or story with this person. In my own way, I will thank this person for being my friend.

Hi, Karen! Boy, what a day I had today! The kids just wouldn't let up!
Too bad!
Nurse! Nurse!
I need my medicine!
Help!

And the paperwork! It's endless!
Must be rough!
IN
NURSE KAREN
OUT

My boss was in a foul mood too!
That's annoying!
EMERGENCY MEETING THIS AFTERNOON ALL STAFF!

Well, I gotta go. Say — how'd your day go?
Fine.

Name________________________________ Date ____________

Good Friends

Worksheet #21

Directions: The following are examples of friends who help promote high self-esteem. Read the stories and identify how the friend is being a positive influence.

1. I was terrified to move to Chicago after having lived in a small town for my entire life. I remember not being able to sleep at all the night before I had to go to my new school. As I was walking to school, I heard footsteps behind me and turned around to see a smiling face. It was a neighbor, Sharon, whom I had briefly met the day we moved in. She walked with me to school, told me she'd meet me at the cafeteria for lunch, and encouraged me to join the Yearbook staff with her. She said she was new to the school last year, and knew what it was like to be new.

   ____

2. My softball team had been doing great all year. During the very last game of the tournament, I struck out. Worst of all, we lost by one run and there were two runners on base when I struck out. I know I didn't lose the game for everyone, but I felt as though it was personally my fault. Juan, a teammate whom I didn't know very well, slapped me on the back and said I had done a good job and not to forget about the home run I had made in the last game.

   ____

3. I got the news that my little brother was hit by a car and was in surgery when I was in my math class, third hour, at school. I was called out of class and came unglued. I just freaked out, screaming and crying. My friend, Kaneesha, who has a car, left school with me in a matter of seconds. She stayed with me at the hospital through the whole ordeal, talking to me, comforting me, and just listening to me. It turned out that my brother was OK, but I'll never forget how much I needed Kaneesha that day and how she came through for me.

   ____

4. Mike and I spent a lot of time working on my dad's old car. I wanted to learn how to make some of the repairs, but my dad didn't have the time – or knowledge – to show me. Mike did. He spent hours with me after school and on weekends, showing me how to use spare parts to get the car to run. He was always patient, teaching me things without making me feel stupid. I think he knew how much I wanted to learn.

   ____

5. Angela and I were close friends during middle school, but kind of drifted apart during high school. One day another person, Dee, started spreading rumors about me; things that weren't nice and certainly weren't true. I found out that Angela approached her, told her she better get her facts straight, and really took up for me. I was pleasantly surprised, especially since we weren't even that close as friends anymore.

   ____

Name________________________________ Date ____________

Could-Be-Better Friends

Worksheet #2[cut off]

Directions: These are some examples of friends you could probably do without. How could th[e] behavior or conversation of each person below affect someone's self-esteem?

1.

Oh, you look fine. Don't change a thing. (Wow! Her hair is really wierd!)

2.

Sure, you can borrow my car. Make sure you get it washed and leave me gas money. This means you have to do my homework for a week.

3.

Sorry your team lost the basketball game. If you had played better, they might have won.

4.

Here comes Tracy. Let's not tell her about the party this weekend. She will want to bring her ugly sister.

5.

Ann has been so stuck-up since she got that job selling clothes. She used to be nice; now she thinks she's better than every-one else. Well, she doesn't seem to have time to talk to me anymore . . . I'm not going to talk to her anymore either!

6.

I told my parents that I spent the weekend with my friend Bob, when I really wasn't there. I expected Bob to back me up on that, but he sure didn't. Boy, did I get in trouble! Some friend! I'm really going to get back at him!

Lesson 11: Peer Groups

People are a part of several groups — the people we work with, play on a team with, join clubs with, and are associated with because of other interests. Belonging to a group is important. It helps us define who we are and influences our thinking.

Objectives

- The student will identify several peer groups of whom he or she is a member.
- The student will identify ways in which a member of a peer group can enhance the self-esteem of another person.

Introduction

1. Have students list the names of three people with whom they have regular contact such as a member of team, youth group, school club, neighbor, or other person who may not particularly be a close friend.
2. Explain that a **peer** is someone who is similar to another person in terms of age (usually within a few years), interests, or in some association.

WORKSHEET #23: WHO ARE YOUR PEERS?

Synopsis: Peers are people who are associated in some way with another in terms of age, grade, or social group. Students are to identify people who are examples of peers.

Directions: Students are to read the examples of peer groups and give an example of what that peer might be saying to the student.

Answers: (examples)

1. Hey! Give me that sweater! 2. Get out of my way. 3. Can you help me with that? 4. May I sit with you? 5. Let's practice after school. 6. Let's work on that painting. 7. Want to go to the mall? 8. Listen to this record.

Discussion Questions:

1. How do your peers influence you? *(the way you dress, things you do)*
2. Do you consider your peers to be your friends?
3. What types of interests draw people together? *(sports, talents, etc.)*

WORKSHEET #24: ROLE-PLAYING SITUATIONS WITH PEERS

Synopsis: Students may react in different ways to the situations in which peers place them. A student with a strong self-esteem may respond to a problem situation without causing further worry, while a student who is unsure of himself or herself might make the situation worse for himself or herself.

Directions: With a partner, students are to devise and present a short role-play in which peers are interacting. The positive situations should achieve some sort of resolution in which the individuals help each other; the negative situations should demonstrate how the students could handle the conflict.

Answers: (examples)

1. Person A could ignore B; A could make a comment such as "Sorry you don't like my taste. Most people think it's cute," etc. 2. Person C could admit that he doesn't understand, while Person D could reassure him that he will be able to catch on. 3. Person F could say, "I really thought you had a good topic. I was curious about what you said. Maybe you could tell me some more about it." 4. Person G could handle H by ignoring him. 5. Person J could offer to help Person I after school if he wants to put in some extra time to learn to play better. 6. Person L could ask the bus driver if there is another seat or try to engage K in normal conversation about school or his interests.

Discussion Questions:

1. Why do you think some people try to cut down others? *(to make themselves feel important or better)*
2. Do the people who put down others have low or high self-esteem? *(low!)*
3. What are some school situations in which a peer has helped improve the self-esteem of another person? *(an athlete, a tutor, a member of a club, etc.)*
4. What are some ways in which peers can resolve conflicts without involving adults, such as a teacher, bus driver, parent, etc.? *(try to talk to each other, ignore each other or try to avoid problem situations, talk to another peer who might be objective)*

Lesson Review

1. Give an example of five peers. Include peers from different groups with which you are involved.
2. Give an example of a way in which a peer has tried to improve your self-esteem.

Journal-Entry Ideas

- What are some groups in which you are involved? What common interests or activities do you participate in that involve peers?
- Which of your peers do you admire? For what reason(s) do you admire this person?
- If a parent, teacher, or other adult advised you to do something, but several members of your peer group told you to do the opposite, what would you do? Under what circumstances would you be more likely to listen to your peers?

Teacher Journal

How do you and your fellow teachers support each other? Are there cliques and factions on your staff? What things draw you together? What things alienate some members?

Goal for the Day

Today I will seek out a peer with whom I have little contact. I will make an effort to find out something about this person and look for something that we have in common. Perhaps today is the day that my colleague needs to hear a kind word or a compliment.

Name________________________________ Date ____________

Who Are Your Peers?

Worksheet #23

Directions: Fill in the conversation bubbles in the cartoons below to give an example of what that person, your peer, might be saying to you.

1. your brother/sister
2. your brother's/sister's friend
3. the person who sits behind you in reading class
4. a person who rides your bus
5. someone who plays on a sports team with you
6. an individual who is in a youth group, church group, or other community group with you
7. your best friend
8. someone who is in an art club, dance club, or other group that meets for fun

Name____ Date ______________

Role-Playing Situations with Peers

Worksheet #2-

Directions: Choose partners and devise a short role-play to perform in front of the class. Use th following situations to get your team started. Don't forget to resolve the situation!

1. **Person A** buys a new, very stylish, very expensive outfit. **Person B** walks by and makes comment about the outfit that are intended to hurt or embarrass Person A.

2. **Person C** is having trouble understanding an assignment in science. **Person D**, who sits nea Person C, offers to help.

3. **Person E** gives a speech in class and was nervous about it. **Person F** gives him/her complimentar feedback about the speech.

4. **Person G** is a loner, someone who keeps to himself/herself most of the time. **Person H** is loud rough, and goes out of his/her way to call attention to Person G.

5. **Person I** is a good athlete. He/she is paired with **Person J**, who is not athletic at all. They are both supposed to practice playing tennis, since they will be partners in a class tournament.

6. **Person K** rides the school bus each morning and afternoon. He/she is usually always getting int trouble, teasing younger riders, throwing things on the bus, and trying to trip people. **Person L** just started riding the bus and has to sit next to Person K.

Lesson 12: Moral and Religious Beliefs

Religion, ethics, and the formation of ideas about right and wrong are all part of our lives and affect not only how we behave but how we feel about ourselves and others. It is important to come to terms with this "philosophy of life," as this reflects our personal values.

Objectives

- The student will be able to explain or define **morality** (right/wrong), **religion** (belief system), and **values** (what is important to someone).
- The student will identify types of situations that reflect making moral decisions.
- The student will be able to state several personal beliefs and give reasons to support these beliefs.

Introduction

Write the words RIGHT and WRONG on the board. Ask students to silently come up with a list of three things they feel are "right" or "good" for others. They should do the same for the "wrong" side. Then have students share their ideas. Informally survey which items seem to appear on most students' lists *(examples:* it is wrong to kill someone; it is right to help the poor, etc.). Acknowledge that it is difficult to categorize many things as entirely "right" or "wrong."

WORKSHEET #25: VALUES, MORALS, RELIGION

Synopsis: Students may already have a good idea of what is entailed in a discussion of values, morals, and religion. By using a general list of strong statements, the worksheet introduces several of these concepts for students to consider and then discuss.

Directions: Students are to read the list of statements. Explain that not everyone values the same things, and although most populations have some standards for rightness and wrongness, there is a lot of room for interpretation. The use of morals or religion is one way in which people learn to test what is right or wrong. Assure students that this is a personal survey, and they are not going to be expected to share more than they feel comfortable with revealing to the class.

Discussion Questions:

1. Why do people value different things, even if they come from the same family? *(depends on their experiences; how they interpret things, personal interests, etc.)*
2. Do you think someone who grew up without a lot of material possessions would consider them important later? *(maybe – but, on the other hand, they may not even desire these things)*
3. Why is it important for there to be standards of right and wrong? *(otherwise it would be a chaotic society; everyone could do anything they wanted, hurt anyone they wanted, have no sense of order or treasuring other people)*
4. How do organized religions help people cope with life? *(teach them right and wrong, show meaning of life, etc.)*
5. Do you think people's ideas of right and wrong change as they grow older? *(probably some things; others might be lifelong beliefs that are constantly true for them)*

WORKSHEET #26: MY CONVICTIONS, MY BELIEFS

Synopsis: Students are to think about their own personal beliefs about morality, values, and religion. Even if these are not shared with the class, it is an opportunity for them to seriously give these concepts some thought.

Directions: Students are given a list of open-ended questions. They are to think about their responses (emphasize "think" before writing down their thoughts) and be prepared to discuss the ones they find interesting, important, or feel strongly about.

Discussion Questions:

Note: You may want to develop some "ground rules" before turning students loose to discuss their opinions. They should respect the comments of others. No "put-downs" should be allowed, especially of others' religious beliefs.

1. Where did you develop your ideas about what is right and wrong?
2. How much of an influence were your parents, your church or religious education, or experiences that you had growing up?
3. How does it make you feel when someone disagrees with you very strongly about something you feel very strongly about? How can you handle this conflict, especially when a friend is involved?
4. Do you think what you do on a day-to-day basis reflects your basic beliefs about life?
5. Are other people aware of your beliefs?
6. Do you think you will change some of your feelings as you experience more of life? *(probably)*
7. If someone didn't believe in the death penalty, but then had a brother murdered by a career criminal, is it possible that the person would change his or her mind about the death penalty? *(possibly)* Why? *(the experience hit home; became real)*

Lesson Review

1. What is a value? Give an example of something that a person would value.
2. What is meant by morality or having morals? Give an example.
3. What is meant by religion? Give an example of a religion.

Journal-Entry Ideas

- What are your feelings about religion? Do you believe there is a God? How is God a part of your life?
- Is your religion or belief system the same as your parents? What influence do you think they have had on you?
- How many different religions can you name? Do you know anything about many of them?
- Make a list of things you believe are always right. Make a list of things you believe are always wrong.
- Do you think it is ever right to kill someone else? Under what circumstances?
- How do you feel about abortion?
- What should be done with people who continually break the rules of society, such as mass murderers, people without a conscience, etc.?
- Have you ever had a discussion or an argument with someone else about religion? How did it make you feel?
- Do you ever think about death? What do you believe awaits you at the end of life?
- Does life have a purpose? Do you ever feel that it all makes sense? What has led you to your conclusions?

Teacher Journal

Think about your own beliefs. Perhaps it has been a while since you evaluated what you really want out of life and believe life is worth. Take a moment to consider what the purpose of your existence is – and what you're going to do with your life today.

Goal for the Day

Don't be afraid to use the words "right" and "wrong" in your class. Today I might have the opportunity to let my students hear some of my beliefs. Maybe I will announce that cheating is "wrong"; or that I am going to pay my taxes because it is the "right" thing to do (although unpopular!); or that it is "wrong" to call someone a racist name.

Middleton School staff experiences a revival.

Name________________________________ Date ______________

Values, Morals, Religion

Worksheet #25

Directions: Read the following statements. Write "A" if you agree with the statement; write "D" if you disagree. If you have mixed feelings, write "M."

_____ 1. There is a God.

_____ 2. There is no God.

_____ 3. Some things are always right.

_____ 4. You should never tell a lie.

_____ 5. Bad things sometimes happen to good people.

_____ 6. You should learn to accept some things that you don't understand.

_____ 7. People should try to get along with each other.

_____ 8. It is wrong to hurt other people.

_____ 9. The most important thing in life is being good.

_____ 10. If you pray, good things will happen to you.

_____ 11. People are basically good.

_____ 12. People are basically evil.

_____ 13. My life has a specific purpose.

_____ 14. It is wrong to commit suicide.

_____ 15. You should always try to do your best.

_____ 16. Our country should do everything it can to help people in underdeveloped countries.

_____ 17. If you want to be left alone, you should be allowed to be left alone.

_____ 18. Once you are 18, your parents shouldn't tell you what to do anymore.

_____ 19. If you borrow money, you should pay it back.

_____ 20. Abortion is OK in some specific circumstances.

Name____ Date ______________

My Convictions, My Beliefs

Worksheet #26

Directions: Think about your own personal beliefs and the basis for your way of thinking. How does your belief system resolve the following issues?

- How do you know what is right and wrong?

  ____

- Are some things always right and some things always wrong? What?

  ____

- What is the meaning of life?

  ____

- What do you think happens when you die?

  ____

- Are some people born "better" than others?

  ____

- How does association with a church or having strong religious beliefs help someone deal with death? pain and suffering? the purpose of life? coping with difficulty?

  ____

- Do you tend to hang around with people who believe similarly to yourself?

  ____

- Could you ever see yourself in a situation in which you would really hurt or kill someone?

  ____

- How do you believe people should treat other people?

  ____

- What is something you strongly believe in that you don't want other people to know about?

  ____

Lesson 13: Life Experiences

Life is a mixture of good and bad experiences. Death, divorce, disease, disabilities, and plain bad luck can taint the view that someone has of life and of his or her place in life. On the other hand, an individual who is healthy, has a loving family, lives a comfortable lifestyle, has won a full scholarship to a college (or won the lottery!) might feel very good about himself or herself. We cannot help but think of our lives in terms of the experiences that have occurred and how they will affect our future.

Objectives

- The student will give examples of significant life events that can affect the individual's perception of life and self-esteem.
- The student will volunteer personal life experiences he or she feels have contributed to his or her current outlook on life and self-esteem.

Introduction

Select a well-known individual to use as an example, perhaps Abraham Lincoln, Thomas Edison, Amelia Earhart, or Ludwig van Beethoven. Read a short biography (perhaps from an encyclopedia entry) of this individual, noting the significant events in this person's life. Emphasize the personal events in the individual's life, rather than his or her achievements. (*For example:* Beethoven's mother died when he was 17, his father was a drunk and was abusive to him, he began losing his hearing when he was in his twenties, etc. Despite these events, he was known as one of the greatest musical composers of all time.) Discuss briefly how these events may have affected the person's outlook on life and his or her self-esteem.

Worksheet #27: Personal Timeline

Synopsis: Students are to work on individual historical autobiographies, emphasizing events that happened in their lives. This can be a personal task, or it can be a general project to be shared with the class. The items on the worksheet are guidelines to suggest ideas or jog memories.

Directions: Students are to read the suggestions for events that have occurred in their lives and to think about what they would like to include on a personal timeline. You may want students to actually construct a timeline, beginning with their birth, including significant events, and ending with the present time. Students may want to include photographs, drawings, and other visuals to make their timelines attractive.

Discussion Questions:

1. Certain events are common to everyone. What are some examples of these? *(walking, talking, starting school, having birthdays, etc.)*
2. When you look back at your life, do you tend to remember the good, the bad, or a mixture of both?
3. How has the effect of time changed your feelings about certain events that happened a long time ago, for example, the death of a parent, perhaps a divorce, moving from a town to the city, saying good-bye to your best friend, etc.? Does time lessen the hurt or pain?
4. Do you think your significant life events are similar to those of many other people? Have you had some experiences you feel are very unique? What are they?

Lesson Review

1. Give three examples of significant life events. Explain how each could affect an individual's self-esteem.
2. Give an example of a personal event that has affected how you feel about yourself today.

Journal-Entry Ideas

- What were the circumstances in your family, city, and the world when you were born? When you picture your entry into the world, what do you envision?
- If you could pick out one special wonderful memory, what would it be? What made it so special?
- Has anyone in your family died unexpectedly or had to deal with a disease? How has that affected others in the family?
- Write a brief autobiography of your life up to now. What events are important to include?

Teacher Journal

What event(s) have helped shape your outlook on life? Do you have feelings of blame towards someone? Are you still holding a grudge? Are you tremendously grateful for something that happened a long time ago that affects you every day of your life?

Goal for the Day

I will view today as another point on my timeline. Today I will look for something outstanding, something significant, something really important to happen. If it doesn't find me, perhaps I will create it myself!

Name________________________________ Date ____________

Personal Timeline

Worksheet #27

Directions: Complete your personal timeline. You may want to include some of the information on the list below. Feel free to add your own!

— when and where I was born

— circumstances of my birth

— my family (siblings, etc.) at the time of my birth

— what happened in the world on the day I was born

— things that my parents remember about me when I was little

— "firsts" (first word, first step, first accident)

— funny things I did when I was little

— places I went

— starting school

— my special friends

— pets

— my favorite things when I was little

— moving to a new house, city, state

— birthdays (pictures?)

— events that I remember (weddings, funerals, special dates, trips)

— summer vacations

— my teachers each year

— things that were happening in the world as I was growing up

— my latest birthday

— my present school, friends, likes/dislikes

Lesson 14: School Experiences

School is a tremendously important experience for most children. Not only are they expected to learn (and follow) rules for socialization, they are also evaluated constantly, corrected, and expected to fit into an often-rigid atmosphere. Some do not understand the expectations that school has for them. Others breeze through and find school to be a rewarding, challenging experience. Although the primary purpose is to receive an education and to be equipped to handle life after school, there are many other skills taught incidentally in this environment.

Objectives

- The student will list three to five skills that are usually taught at school and give an example of each.
- The student will identify ways in which a positive or a negative school experience can affect an individual's self-esteem.

Introduction

Have students take out a blank sheet of paper. Instruct them to write the word SCHOOL at the top. They are not to put their names on their papers. Then give them 60 seconds to write anything that comes to mind. When students have finished, collect the papers and discuss some of the comments. Are they primarily positive or negative? Any common themes?

Worksheet #28: School Days

Synopsis: Students who sometimes start out well in the early grades lose their enthusiasm, drive, and support to continue to do well. Sadly, it is often lack of self-esteem that gives students the permission to excuse themselves from school rules, attending school, and even seeing how an education can benefit them later.

Directions: Students are to read the story about a student who started out well in school, but eventually dropped out. There are discussion questions on the worksheet pertaining to the story. Students are to write or discuss the questions at the end.

Answers (examples):

1. He couldn't wait to go; it seemed like it would be a fun place to go. 2. They praised his drawings, displayed his work, etc. 3. His teacher asked him to make a drawing for her. 4. He started getting into trouble and did not finish his work. He seemed to feel that the work was getting harder. 5. It sounds like Kameel did not try very hard, nor did most of the teachers particularly want to work with Kameel. 6. He thought he was too much of a problem for the teachers to want to deal with for more than one year. 7. The industrial arts teacher spent extra time with him and got him a job; he was in a class for at-risk kids in high school. 8. He will probably drop out of school and find a low-paying job.

Worksheet #29: School and Self-Esteem

Synopsis: School experiences can directly affect how an individual feels about himself or herself. If a student hears praise, is able to withstand a challenge, and learns lessons well, he or she will probably feel good about himself or herself and view school as something he or she can endure. If a student struggles daily with work, is not accepted by peers, is a problem for teachers, and does not do well academically, school will probably make him or her feel even worse about himself or herself.

Directions: Students are to match the school experience listed on the left with an example of how that experience occurs on the right. Students can put the letter of the example on the line.

Answers: 1. d; 2. c; 3. h; 4. f; 5. b; 6. g; 7. e; 8. a

Discussion Questions:

1. Is being "evaluated" a pleasant experience sometimes? How? *(yes, if you know that your work is good and it's an opportunity to be praised)*
2. Are there some students who will never do well in a traditional school setting? Why? *(too many rules; too structured; teachers won't "bend" for them; etc.)*
3. Do you think everyone should be forced to stay in school, at least through high school? *(opinions may vary!)*
4. Do you think everyone in society should at least be steered toward getting a job, even if they don't finish high school?
5. Can you think of some examples of people who have been successful without getting a high school education? *(Dave Thomas, founder of* ***Wendy's*** *restaurant, for example)*
6. What values are taught at school? *(self-control; quality of products; getting along with others; care of property; etc.)*

Lesson Review

1. What are some skills taught at school? Give an example and describe if it is academic, social, behavioral, etc.
2. Give an example of how a bad school experience could shape a student into having a low self-esteem.
3. Give an example of how a good school experience could shape a student into having a high self-esteem.

Journal-Entry Ideas

- Can you list the names of all the teachers you have had since you started school? Which ones stand out in your mind? Why?
- Who was/is your favorite teacher? Why?
- If you could change three things about school to make it better, what would they be?
- Do you think graduating from high school is important? Why or why not?

Teacher Journal

You represent the school to many students. You evaluate them, correct them, teach them. If you could teach only one concept, one idea, one rule today . . . what would it be?

Goal for the Day

Today I will stand outside my door or in the hallway before students enter my classroom. I will greet each one by name as they come in. Maybe I will even say, "Welcome to my classroom. I've got some great learning in store for you today."

You know what? If your standards are low enough, everyone can be successful!
Yeah, I thought about giving points for participation to my afternoon class for keeping their eyes open and breathing without snoring.

Name____ Date ______________

School Days

Worksheet #28

Directions: Read the following story about Kameel and his experiences in school. Then answer the questions on page 2.

"I couldn't wait to start school when I was little. My older sister and brother went off to school and I remember watching them through the window, hardly able to wait until I could go.

"My first few years were great. I loved to draw and had teachers who praised my drawings. My first-grade teacher used to hang my pictures on the bulletin board for everyone to see. One time she asked me to make a haunted house with jack-o'-lanterns around it for a school program. I was so proud.

"When I got to third grade, it seemed like there was so much work to do that I never had time to draw. I would make the time, though. During math or reading when I was supposed to be working, I would be illustrating my worksheets with horses, monsters, or airplanes. My teacher liked my drawings, but told me to finish my work first and then I could have time to draw. But I lost interest in school. The work got harder and I didn't want to have to work that hard.

"I started getting into trouble in class. I would make noises, tease other kids, and never finish my work. Teachers would try so hard to get me to take work home, but once I got home – well, there was no way I was going to do homework. There was basketball to play, bikes to ride, and friends to hang out with. My friends weren't that interested in school either.

"My parents tried to work with me. In fact, my mother hired a tutor to try to help me catch up with my work. I liked working one to one with her, but it didn't help me at school. I kept getting further and further behind. I just couldn't seem to keep up with all of the work. It seemed hopeless.

"I was such a nuisance that the teachers kept passing me on to the next grade. I had a few in middle school who liked me and tried to work with me. My industrial arts teacher was really cool. He showed me how to use the machines to work with wood. In fact, he got me a part-time job after school cutting out wood pieces for another teacher to use with her class. I liked him a lot. He really seemed to care about me. He would always ask me questions about what I was interested in and what I liked to do. He was also the track coach and tried to talk me into trying out for the team, but I didn't want to put the time into practices.

"By the time I got to high school (believe it or not, I made it), I got put into a special class for kids who are headed for dropping out. I think the teachers in that program were really nice, but I got turned off by having to do work. Sometimes they'd take us on trips to community places where we could do odd jobs and learn about possible careers. That was fun. But when we got back, they always wanted us to write in a journal about what we did and what we thought.

"School became more and more boring. I knew if I stayed that I would continue to get into trouble. I just can't sit at a desk. It drives me crazy. My parents said that I could drop out as long as I could get a job somewhere. My uncle works in a factory and said that they might be hiring in the spring. If I can get a job there, I'm going."

Discussion Questions

1. What were Kameel's earliest impressions of school?

2. How did the teachers affect his self-esteem when he was in elementary school?

3. What important memory did Kameel have in first grade?

4. Why did Kameel grow less interested in school as he got older?

5. Do you blame Kameel or the teachers for his lack of success in school?

6. Why did Kameel believe he was passed on from grade to grade?

7. What attempts were made to help Kameel stay in school and succeed?

8. What do you see in the future for Kameel?

Name____ Date ______________

School and Self-Esteem

Worksheet #29

Directions: Match the school experience on the left with an example of that experience on the right. Put the letter on the blank.

_____ 1. In school, you are evaluated by others.

_____ 2. If you do really well, your peers might make fun of you.

_____ 3. If you fail, you will get in trouble with teachers and administrators.

_____ 4. School can be a very stressful experience for students.

_____ 5. At school, we learn the values of our community and our culture.

_____ 6. You always have to prove yourself to someone or they won't believe you or respect you.

_____ 7. It is important to hear praise once in a while so you don't give up.

_____ 8. School is a place for you to learn survival skills for the future.

a. You can take classes in bookkeeping, typing, and career preparation.

b. There is a book of rules for students to follow at school. It includes a dress code, penalties for not following the rules, and a list of clubs and activities to join.

c. Marsha was given the nickname "Brain" because of her good grades.

d. Your assignments and homework are graded by teachers.

e. Sometimes teachers select a student of the week to receive a reward or honor.

f. There is pressure to complete work, get good grades, and test well enough to get into college.

g. Even in high school you have to have things signed by your parents.

h. Henry could not try out for sports because of his low grades.

Lesson 15: Work Experiences

Attaining and holding down a job can give an individual a sense of worth and accomplishment, as well as a steady paycheck. A pleasant work experience can lead to security, social relationships with coworkers, and give the individual a sense of power over his or her life. On the other hand, persons who are unskilled, unable to hold a job, or uninterested in becoming part of the work force may feel quite the opposite.

Objective

- The student will state at least three positive outcomes from work or career experiences.

Introduction

Have students list several jobs or careers that would satisfy the following descriptions:

– a job that is dangerous

– a job that pays well

– a job that requires a lot of skill

– a job that has flexible hours

– a job that is primarily outdoors

– a job that involves a lot of sitting down

– a job that involves writing

Worksheet #30: Positive Work Experiences

Synopsis: A positive work experience can contribute to building a high self-esteem. Comments and praise from others on the job can be gratifying; monetary rewards and benefits can lead to a better standard of living; and job security can contribute to peace of mind.

Directions: Students are to read the comments by workers, coworkers, and other related personnel on the job. They are to decide how each comment or event would lead to a higher self-esteem for the worker involved.

Answers (examples):

1. Boss is complimentary to the worker, who would probably feel good about himself. 2. The worker feels a sense of importance and need to be on the job. 3. The worker has a good relationship with a coworker who is helpful and supportive. 4. The worker is managing his money well and planning to make needed purchases. 5. The worker is secure in his job. 6. The coworker is inviting the worker to join in leisure activities, making her feel part of a group.

Discussion Questions:

1. How can a good or a bad relationship with a boss affect someone's job?
2. How can a good or a bad relationship with coworkers affect a job?
3. What are some benefits to doing a job well?
4. Do you think most people would work as well if they weren't supervised or aware of a boss looking over their shoulder?
5. Why do you think some people try to avoid work or are not interested in performing well on the job?
6. What types of jobs or career-exploration activities are available to you? How could you find out more about certain careers?

Lesson Review

1. List three benefits to having a job or career.
2. Give an example of how your three benefits listed above can help develop an individual's self-esteem.

Journal-Entry Ideas

- When you were little, what did you want to be when you were grown up? Why were you interested in that job?
- What career or jobs interest you now? Why?
- What career or jobs do your parents have? Do you have any interest in doing something similar?

Teacher Journal

On the days when you think about not being a teacher, what careers interest you? What would you have been if you didn't go into teaching? If you have an additional job, what is it? How do your other interests affect how you teach?

Goal for the Day

Today I will take a moment to talk to my students about why I became a teacher. I will reassure them that it was a choice and that I am here because I want to be here. I will consciously make sure that my actions match my comments today.

Name________________________________ Date ____________

Positive Work Experiences

Worksheet #3C

Directions: Read the following comments from workers, supervisors, coworkers, and other work personnel. Decide how each can contribute to a positive self-esteem.

1. You are doing an excellent job, Tony. I can trust you to get the job done without constant supervision. You're headed for a promotion soon!

2. It's 7:00. It seems so early to get up, but I'm really needed on the job. If I'm not there, it won't be done right.

3. If I don't know how to do something, I go to Sarah. She's good at explaining things and never makes me feel stupid, especially when I know the boss is going to be coming around to check.

4. I love getting a paycheck. After I pay my bills, I'll have enough left over to start saving up for a new car.

5. My brother lost his job last week. I'm really glad that my job is secure. I can count on having that paycheck and that work.

6. Hey, Alicia – are you going to join the company's bowling team? We really have a lot of fun on Friday nights!

Lesson 16: The Media

Look through a magazine for a moment and notice the ads you see, or pay attention to the products and services advertised on the radio. How many have to do with becoming better looking, more successful, buying smarter, having a nicer car, or finding an attorney to get you out of something? It is hard for any typical person to live up to the standard that seems to be held out for us according to the media.

Objectives

- The student will summarize the intent or implied message of an advertisement on radio, TV, or newspaper.
- The student will evaluate product or service messages from advertisements.

Introduction

Have students bring in pictures of their favorite ads and display them around the room or take an informal class survey of popular ads. Allow student volunteers time to practice performing a commercial for an ad and present it to the class. Creative students may want to write their own ads, perhaps doing a parody of a well-known commercial.

Worksheet #31: Messages from the Media

Synopsis: Media ads for products to make us look better, smell better, be popular, etc., are easy to locate in newspapers, radio ads, and magazine ads. Other media sources are billboards, posters on bulletin boards, and even signs on buses. Students are to observe ads and decide what the bottom-line message is to the public.

Directions: Examples of products or services available (and promoted) to the public are listed on the worksheet. Students are to think of where these ads would be found and then to list an example of a media message presented from the ad.

Answers (examples):

1. If you use this perfume, you will attract good-looking men. 2. If you smoke this brand of cigarette, you will appear to be rugged and tough. 3. These jeans will make you popular. 4. If you work out, you will have a fantastic body. 5. This cereal will give you energy. 6. This equipment is easy to use and will help you lose weight. 7. This shampoo will make your hair shine. 8. Everyone wears these tennis shoes. 9. This ice cream will help you stay thin. 10. These diet pills will make you skinny in a short time. 11. If you drive this sports car, you will be successful. 12. If you have a headache, you need to take some sort of medication.

Discussion Questions:

1. Do you think most people believe the messages that are given to us?
2. Do you think most people are concerned about looking good, being successful, having nice possessions, and being attractive to others? *(to some extent, yes . . . but most people probably aren't so obsessed with these ideas as the ads would make you think)*
3. Would you buy a particular product because you liked the commercial?
4. How does it make you feel when you see ads promoting expensive clothing? Do you want to buy those products?

Worksheet #32: Evaluating Media Messages

Synopsis: Students are given a list of questions to assist them in evaluating the messages that ads or commercials are promoting. They are to think critically about who the commercial is for, think about the validity of the ad, and decide whether or not it is effective.

Directions: Students are to find and use an example of a product or service that is advertised and then evaluate the message using the list of questions on the worksheet.

Lesson Review

1. List three current ads or commercials for products or services.
2. Write the stated or implied message of each of the ads you selected.
3. Evaluate the message of each of the ads you selected. Is it a good ad? Is it accurate? Does it make you want to buy the product or service?

Journal-Entry Ideas

- How important is it to you to wear name-brand clothing? Do you think kids are labeled or grouped according to the clothes they wear?
- What types of ads or commercials do you find offensive or embarrassing?
- What products or services have you recently bought as a direct result of a commercial or ad? Were you happy with what you got?
- If you could invent a pill to change something about yourself, what do you wish would be changed?
- Write an ad or commercial to promote the product you would invent.

Teacher Journal

Write an ad or commercial for a learning unit you are presently working on with your class. How can you entice students to become involved in learning what you are teaching? What's in it for them? How can you make it more attractive? Why do they need to learn what you are teaching?

Goal for the Day

Instead of complimenting students on their expensive clothes or new haircut, I will concentrate on giving compliments to students based on things I like about them that don't involve buying specialized media products. It's easy to say, "I want you to know I have noticed how friendly you are to everyone," "Your hair looks nice today," "I found some interesting ideas in your paragraph," or "It's great that you jog every day after school." These are all things that any student can do, but don't involve being enticed into a false image of what he or she is supposed to look like, act, or be.

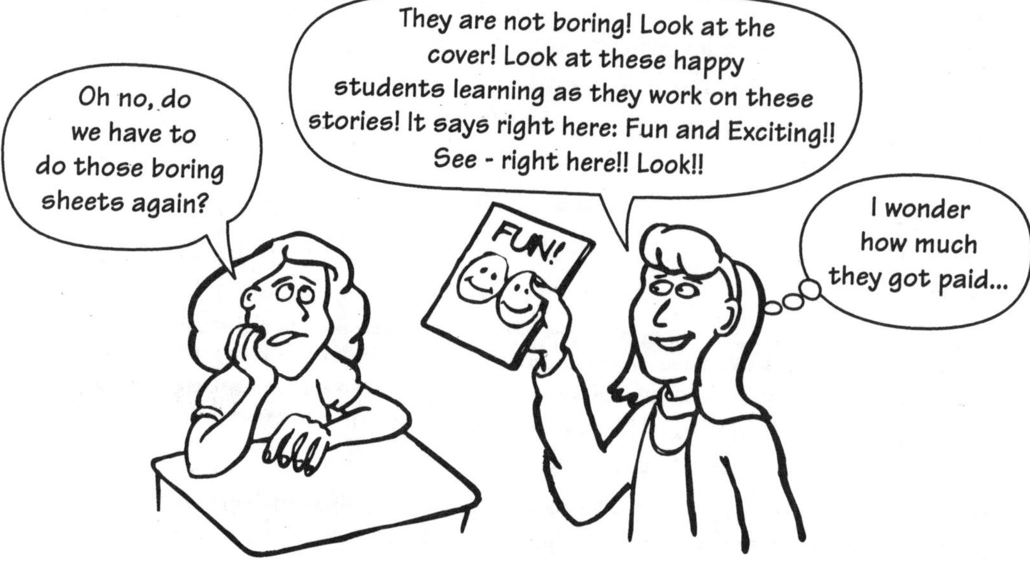

Name______________________________ Date __________

Messages from the Media

Worksheet #31

Directions: How are the following products or services advertised to the general public? What messages are given through these commercial ads?

1. perfume ______________________________
____
2. cigarettes ______________________________
____
3. jeans ______________________________
____
4. health club ______________________________
____
5. cereal ______________________________
____
6. exercise equipment ______________________________
____
7. shampoo ______________________________
____
8. name-brand tennis shoes ______________________________
____
9. low-fat ice cream ______________________________
____
10. diet pills ______________________________
____
11. sports car ______________________________
____
12. headaches ______________________________
____

Name____ Date ______________

Evaluating Media Messages

Worksheet #32

Directions: Find an example of an interesting product or service that is advertised on television, the radio, newspaper, magazine, or other source. Evaluate the message by answering the following questions:

1. What product or service is being promoted?

   ____

2. Who is the target audience for this product or service?

   ____

3. What attitude does the advertiser have? For example, is it trying to take care of you, show you how to have fun or be popular, educate you, etc.?

   ____

4. What technique or techniques are used to get your attention?

   ____

5. How effective do you think this advertisement is? Does it make you want to buy something or do something?

   ____

6. Complete the following sentence according to the ad: If you buy this product or engage in this service, you will . . .

   ____

7. How much effect do you think this ad has on the general public?

   ____

8. How would this particular ad affect people who are easily influenced and tend to believe that whatever they see, hear, or read is probably true?

   ____

9. How would this ad affect people who like themselves, are confident, but are willing to evaluate new experiences and products?

   ____

10. How does this ad make you feel?

   ____

Lesson 17: Talents, Abilities, Personality Traits

An individual seems to have it all – good looks, athletic ability, outgoing personality, intelligence . . . yet such a person could surprisingly be insecure, fearful, and full of self-doubts. Nevertheless, when a person takes inventory of his or her unique characteristics, if he or she feels there are some positive talents, abilities, and desired personality traits, this can prove to be a good foundation for building a positive self-esteem.

Objectives

- The student will identify examples of talents and abilities that are thought of as desirable.
- The student will identify examples of personality traits that are thought of as desirable.
- The student will identify personal examples of positive talents, abilities, and personality traits.

Introduction

Ask students to take out a piece of paper and write down one word they feel describes himself or herself. When students are finished, have them raise their hand to indicate into which category their descriptive word falls: what they can *do*; what they *are*. (You might want to further try to find a trend of male vs. female responses–is it true that males think abilities are more important than personality and females have the reverse attitude?)

WORKSHEET #33: YOUR TALENTS AND ABILITIES

Synopsis: Having and recognizing a talent or special ability can enhance someone's self-esteem. Students are to think of things that they can do that are positive talents and/or abilities.

Directions: Students are to read the suggested list of talents and abilities on the worksheet. They are then to compile a list of their own talents/abilities.

Discussion Questions:

1. Is there anyone who insists he or she does not possess any talents or abilities? Is this possible? *(probably there will be at least one, but most people can identify something they are capable of doing)*
2. Do you think people are born with certain talents or abilities? Give examples. *(some people seem to be naturally athletic or find it easy to learn how to play an instrument, etc.)*
3. Do you think people can learn to develop a talent or ability? How? *(yes: taking lessons, observing others, giving something a try, etc.)*
4. Why do you think people admire others who are good athletes or excel at something? *(perhaps we wish we could be that good at something; athletes have a special status when they are part of a team and are an essential part of winning)*
5. Could someone who has a lot of talent have a low self-esteem? Explain. *(Yes: they may not value that talent, others around them may not value that talent, they may not be aware of how good they are, etc.)*

WORKSHEET #34: YOUR PERSONALITY CHARACTERISTICS

Synopsis: Some people are outgoing; others are shy. Some have short tempers; others are easy-going. While to some extent personality traits are part of what makes an individual an individual, it is possible to make changes in the way we come across to others, react to others, and handle ourselves.

Directions: Students are to describe their personality. The list on the worksheet can get students started. This differs from the previous worksheet in that the emphasis is on how the student feels about himself or herself, rather than what he or she can do well.

Discussion Questions:

1. Was it easy or difficult to come up with many descriptive phrases for yourself?
2. If you had a close friend look over your list, would he or she agree with your conclusions?
3. Do you think it is more important to be good at something or to be a good person who may not have many talents? Explain. *(opinions may differ)*
4. Can some people have both? *(yes – the lucky ones!)*
5. How could someone change a personality characteristic that he or she doesn't like? *(make a conscious effort to change; take voice lessons; role-play situations; take an assertive training course; etc.)*
6. Is it necessary to make personality changes? For what reason? *(people who struggle with a bad temper may wish to learn to get it under control for social and work reasons; shy people may get further ahead if they become more assertive in business situations; people who blurt out their first thoughts may benefit in the long run from learning to think first, then speak, etc.)*

Lesson Review

1. Give an example of a talent, ability, and personality trait that are thought of as desirable by others.
2. Give an example of a talent, ability, and personality trait you possess that are thought of as desirable by others.

Journal-Entry Ideas

- Look over your list of talents and abilities. Which accomplishments do you attribute to hard work? Which are the result of your natural skills?
- Look over your list of personality characteristics. Put a * next to those personality characteristics you are pleased with. Put a — next to those you wish were different in some way. Why do you feel this way?
- If you could change places for a month with one person (specify living or dead, real or fictional), who would it be? Why?
- Do you want people to know about your talents and abilities or do you prefer to keep them private?

Teacher Journal

What do you feel is your best talent, ability, and personality characteristic? Do others know about your talents? Are you proud of yourself? How does your personality characteristic manifest itself at work? around your friends/family? Do you like yourself?

GOAL FOR THE DAY

Today I will share a little of myself with others. Perhaps I will draw a picture, toss a ball, reveal that I won an award for something, or maybe just allow myself to be louder, funnier, or more of what I tone down or change to fit a certain role. I will watch for the reaction of others.

Name____ Date ______________

Your Talents and Abilities

Worksheet #33

Directions: Make a list of the specific talents and abilities you feel you possess. You may wish to start with some of the ideas listed below, but feel free to add your own.

- play the piano or other musical instrument
- be a good singer
- able to draw well
- good at fixing machines that are broken
- able to type fast
- know how to work computers
- fast runner
- good at gymnastics
- able to train dogs to learn tricks
- handle horses well
- like to do woodworking and use tools
- good at painting pictures
- good at sports, other athletic tasks
- work puzzles well
- enjoy taking pictures
- enjoy performing in plays
- good ballet dancer
- always win at chess or Monopoly®
- put models together
- have a collection of something
- good at saving money (or managing money)

Name____ Date ____________

Your Personality Characteristics

Worksheet #34

Directions: Describe your own unique personality characteristics. Think about what you feel you are like. Use the following ideas to get you started. Come up with at least 20 descriptive phrases about yourself.

- well-organized with time and papers
- hard worker
- have a good sense of humor
- loyal to friends
- respectful of others
- good at following directions
- good at giving directions to others
- good leader
- control of temper
- good listener
- can persuade others to see a different point of view
- willing to help others
- like to work hard
- like to do new things, take on a challenge
- enjoy travelling to new places
- enjoy solving puzzles
- good at remembering messages for others
- enjoy reading for pleasure
- able to understand the needs of older people
- do my share when given a group job
- am outgoing with people, enjoy talking to others
- like to think about things before I make a decision
- appreciate different kinds of music
- have friends of both sexes
- get along well with my parents and family
- am a good older brother/sister
- am responsible when given a job
- forgive others, don't hold a grudge
- can see the "other" side of bad situations
- am good at teaching others how to do something
- like to be around people
- enjoy learning new things

Lesson 18: A Lifetime Process

Factors that influence self-esteem can change over a lifetime—a child becomes a parent, a student becomes a worker, tragedy strikes, success is earned, and attitudes can change—as people experience life events and determine their reaction to them. Maintaining a healthy, strong self-esteem is a process that continues throughout life.

Objectives

- The student will list several factors that can affect a change in one's self-esteem over a lifetime.
- The student will give examples of how several of these factors can help develop a positive self-esteem in an individual.
- The student will give examples of how several of these factors can lead to a negative self-esteem in an individual.

Introduction

Have students think about what was important to them five years ago (e.g., doing well in school, having a best friend, etc.). Then focus on what is important right now. Shift the focus again to what concerns will be most important five years from now (e.g., having a job, making money, etc.). Although the factors will vary among students, there will probably be some commonalities. Ask students why there will be such changes, especially between the ten-year span.

Worksheet #35: Changes Over Time

Synopsis: Students are given a list of factors that probably will have endured changes over time. Their role in a family, for example, will probably be very different in the future. They are to consider how these changes will personally affect them.

Directions: Students are to complete a chart indicating how a specific factor might change over time (from child to present time to future).

Discussion Questions:

1. Which areas do you think involve the most change? *(family, friends, peers, etc.)* Why?
2. Which areas might be the most stable? *(possibly values / religion, talents / abilities, personality)*
3. Do you think if someone has a strong self-esteem as a child that he or she will continue to have a strong self-esteem as an adult? *(it might depend on what life experiences he / she has, how he / she copes with them, etc.)*
4. If a person has a low self-esteem as a child, especially in the area of school, how could this affect him/her later, particularly after his or her school days are over? *(he / she may feel better about self if work is a more successful experience than school was)*

Worksheet #36: Lifetime Changes

Synopsis: Many life events can cause difficulty for individuals. Students are given an opportunity to consider some typical situations and offer advice.

Directions: Students are given examples of individuals who are dealing with difficult situations. They are to make suggestions for how the individual could take steps to make positive changes.

Answers (examples):

1. Antonio could start looking for job possibilities, make sure he finishes high school, try to arrange for his own space, etc. 2. Amy could make it clear that she does not wish to participate in those kinds of activities with them, start making new friends, etc. 3. Rolando could make his values clear to the friend and look for new, more healthy activities for them to do. 4. Patricia

could work on her hair and makeup, shop at specialty stores where they have attractive clothing for larger sizes, and maybe join a diet organization (after talking with her doctor) if this would help her lose weight. 5. David could seek counseling from a minister or other trained person, make sure he has a support system for himself, make time for himself to do things he enjoys, etc. 6. Calisse could talk to a counselor, check out some self-help books, teach herself some control techniques to use with other people, etc.

Discussion Questions:

1. Can you think of any examples of people you know (no names, please) who have turned a bad event into something they could deal with? Explain.
2. It sounds easy to say, "Find new friends," but this is a difficult thing, especially when you are tightly involved in a peer group. What are some ways to get out of an uncomfortable situation involving people who are your friends?
3. Some events—death, disease, etc.—are truly tragic. What are some ways people deal with grief in an unhealthy way? What are some ways people can cope with these tragedies?

Worksheet #37: Role Changes

Synopsis: Roles change over time. A child may become a parent, a student may become a worker, a family might move to a new city involving a change of friends and peers, and so on. As roles change, so self-esteem can change as the individual adapts or fails to adapt successfully to this new role.

Directions: Students are to read the examples and identify what particular factor was involved in a role change for the individual. They are then to consider how this change might affect the person's self-esteem.

Answers (examples):

1. Roberto is now a father; might be proud of this or feel resentful. 2. Michelle has to deal with a tragic life event; this might give her strength to rely on new resources. 3. Linda develops a new talent; this might cause her to feel proud of herself and ready to take a risk. 4. Tim is going to be a brother; may resent having to share his parents with a baby and probably having to baby-sit for the new child. 5. Alex is facing a major life experience; he may be fearful of fitting into a new peer group. 6. Jamine has survived a tragedy and is now focusing her life on religious values. 7. Gerald is having problems with school experiences; might be convinced that he is stupid and feel badly about himself. 8. Kara's friends affected her; she might develop a new talent. 9. Marlin was approached by peers; might reaffirm his values to stay out of trouble. 10. Terry had a new work experience; might affect later career decisions.

Discussion Questions:

1. Are all changes in life bad? *(of course not, a lot depends on the individual's outlook towards the event)*
2. Which of these changes are normal or occur in almost any individual's life? *(friendship changes, peer group, family role and status, moving, change from school to work role, etc.)*

Lesson Review

1. List at least five factors that can affect someone's self-esteem over a lifetime.
2. Give an example of how those factors can affect someone in a positive way.
3. Give an example of how those factors can affect someone in a negative way.

Journal-Entry Ideas

- Have you ever moved to a new house, city, or state? How did the move make you feel? What events surrounding or causing the move affected how you felt about the move?
- Have you ever had to deal with a family or personal tragedy? What was it and how did you react to it? If it was a long time ago, have your feelings about the event changed in any way?
- Do you consider yourself basically a positive person who views things in a positive light? Or do you tend to look at things in a more careful way, thinking about the negative possibilities of a situation?

Teacher Journal

What one single event in the past year or two has affected you and your outlook on life more than anything else?

Goal for the Day

Today when the minor aggravations of the day bother me, I will remember to put it into perspective. Life has ups and downs, and if this is something that will probably pass, I will mentally put it into a little box, store it for a little while, take it out and examine it later to see if it's worth holding on to.

Name________________________________ Date ______________

Changes Over Time

Worksheet #35

Directions: How have these factors changed since you were a child? How do you think these things might affect you in the future? Complete the following chart with your ideas:

Factor:	Child	Now	Future
1. Family	______	______	______
2. Friends	______	______	______
3. Peers	______	______	______
4. Religion/Values	______	______	______
5. Life Experiences	______	______	______
6. Work Experiences	______	______	______
7. Media	______	______	______
8. My Talents/Abilities	______	______	______
9. My Personality	______	______	______
10. School Experiences	______	______	______

Name_______________________________________ Date ________

Lifetime Changes

Worksheet #36

Directions: Each of the following individuals has had difficulty dealing with a factor in his or he life, leading to a poor self-esteem. What could you recommend to help each person make a positive lif change?

1. ANTONIO is 17 and not quite ready to live on his own, but he does not get along well with hi family. There is always a lot of fighting, turmoil, and lack of organization. What could he do t think about making life changes that will help him become independent?

   ____

   ____

2. AMY has a group of friends who are a lot of fun, but more and more they are getting into trouble In fact, what started as shoplifting for excitement has become a regular weekend activity. Am feels uncomfortable about what her friends are leading her into. What could she do to feel she is in control of her activities?

   ____

   ____

3. ROLANDO and his best friend always participated in sports together. His friend is becoming heavily involved in recreational drugs and doing a lot of drinking. Rolando does not agree with this; in fact, he feels it is wrong and does not want any part of it. Still, he wants to remain friends with this boy. What could he do to maintain his own standards?

   ____

   ____

4. PATRICIA has been overweight for most of her life. She wishes she could wear clothes that would make her more attractive. She's thought about crash-dieting, pills, and even exercising to try to lose weight, but she can't stick to anything for very long. What could Patricia do to be more comfortable with the way she looks?

   ____

   ____

5. DAVID lost his father to cancer and was devastated by this tragedy. He feels a tremendous amount of sadness, not to mention a lot of pressure on his family to cope with this loss. What could David do to handle this critical period of his life?

   ____

   ____

6. CALISSE has always had a bad temper. People tend to avoid her because she won't listen and overreacts to everything. Although she realizes this is a problem, she doesn't know what to do other than to blame other people. What could Calisse do if she really wants to change this situation?

   ____

   ____

Name________________________________ Date ____________

Role Changes

Worksheet #37

Directions: What factor (family, friends, peers, religion, life experiences, school experiences, work experiences, media, personal talents) has changed for the following individuals? How would this make a change in the individual's self-esteem?

1. Roberto got his girlfriend pregnant and is planning to get married and become a father.

   ____

   ____

2. Michelle found out she has a rare heart disorder. ________________

   ____

3. Linda began taking violin lessons and found that she really enjoys them and is going to join a community orchestra.

   ____

   ____

4. Tim's mother is going to have a baby. ________________

   ____

5. Alex moved to a new school in another part of the country.

   ____

   ____

6. Jamine survived an awful car accident and decided that God has spared her life. She has decided to become more involved in the church and finding out about religion.

   ____

   ____

7. Gerald is not doing well in school and wants to quit.

   ____

   ____

8. Kara's friends convinced her to play tennis and she realized it was really fun.

   ____

   ____

9. Marlin was approached by some gang members in his school and decided that he wanted no part of them or their activities.

   ____

   ____

10. Terry got a part-time summer job working at a newspaper office and was intrigued by how much was involved in putting together a newspaper. He decided to pursue this as a possible career.

    ____

    ____

Part III

Combatting a Low Self-Esteem

This collection of twenty-two lessons and twenty-four worksheets deals with effective interventions for a specific emotion or situation, such as "What Others Say and Do" and "School and Self-Esteem." Upon completing this section, students are equipped with many ideas on how to combat low self-esteem.

Lesson 19: Taking a Personal Inventory

One way to informally assess the status of one's self-esteem is by examining self-comments. In this lesson, a list of comments an individual might make or agree with can help determine which areas might reflect a low self-esteem.

Objective

- The student will complete a personal inventory in which he or she selects statements that reflect areas of low self-esteem.

Introduction

1. Have students complete the following sentences:

   I don't like my . . .

   I feel badly when . . .

   I wish . . .

   I hate it when I think about . . .

   No one else . . .

2. Ask students to volunteer their responses if they desire to share them with the class. Conclude that everyone has bad days and negative perceptions of themselves at times. The comments we make about ourselves, especially on a constant or consistent basis, are clues to how we feel about ourselves.

Worksheet #38: Personal Inventory

Synopsis: Students are to complete a personal inventory sheet of negative self-comments. By selecting the ones they feel are typical comments they would make, students can start to focus on some areas in which they might need to examine and boost their self-esteem.

Directions: Students are to put a check mark in front of the comments they feel often, or usually, describe themselves. They should write "S" in front of the statements that sometimes describe them.

Discussion Questions:

1. Do you see any patterns to the comments you marked? Are most of the comments dealing with other people, abilities, attitude, etc.?
2. Could you think of specific examples for some of the statements (e.g., a particular person you have a grudge against, a specific bad experience, etc.)?
3. Do you wish you could change some of your responses or do you feel, "That's just the way I am"?
4. Do you believe you can make changes in your life to change how you feel about yourself?

Lesson Review

1. List two or three self-statements that reflect your feelings about yourself on a usual basis.
2. List two or three self-statements that reflect your feelings about yourself on an occasional basis.

Journal-Entry Ideas

- Does anyone (a friend or parent, for example) tell you, "Quit being so negative about yourself"? What specifically are they referring to? What do other people hear you say about yourself when you are talking?

- Do you feel that overall you have a low self-esteem? In which areas of your self-concept do you feel your self-esteem is the lowest?
- Did taking the personal inventory make you feel sad or depressed because it was so negative? Why?

Teacher Journal

What types of self-statements do you make in front of your class and colleagues? If asked, what would your peers probably say about the way you talk about yourself? Are you happy with the image they have perceived about you?

Goal for the Day

Today I will be conscious of how I respond to negative self-statements I hear my students (or colleagues) make. Am I too sympathetic? Do I give the response that the student is looking for (sympathy, reality check, etc.)? I will try to tune in to what that person is expecting as a reaction and decide whether or not I want to provide that response.

Name____ Date ______________

Personal Inventory

Worksheet #38

Directions: Put a check mark in front of each statement below that you feel describes yourself or a comment that you **often** make about yourself. Put an "S" if this describes you **sometimes.**

_____ 1. I don't have any control over what I do.

_____ 2. I don't like myself.

_____ 3. I have no talents or abilities.

_____ 4. I am often depressed.

_____ 5. I know that bad things will happen to me.

_____ 6. I don't like the way I look.

_____ 7. I don't like other people.

_____ 8. I really don't care what happens to me.

_____ 9. I don't ever think about who or what I am.

_____ 10. There are so many things wrong with me.

_____ 11. I can't handle changes.

_____ 12. No one else has problems like mine.

_____ 13. Other people don't like my friends.

_____ 14. I am not important.

_____ 15. Everything is always my fault.

_____ 16. I am always getting my feelings hurt.

_____ 17. I can't stop thinking about bad things happening to me.

_____ 18. Someone is always better than I am.

_____ 19. I am a perfectionist.

_____ 20. I tend to look at the bad side of things.

_____ 21. I can't accept a compliment.

_____ 22. I can't control my emotions.

_____ 23. I will never do well in school.

_____ 24. Other people don't like me.

_____ 25. I can't seem to finish anything.

_____ 26. I always have to be right.

_____ 27. I can't make decisions.

_____ 28. I'm always finding fault with other people.

_____ 29. I'm afraid of rejection.

_____ 30. I get discouraged easily.

_____ 31. I hold grudges against others.

_____ 32. I do things I know will get me into trouble.

_____ 33. I don't deserve to have anything nice.

_____ 34. I can't get along with other people.

_____ 35. I constantly need approval.

Lesson 20: Making Changes: Resources and Planning

To attack the problem of dealing with a low self-esteem, an individual must be able to identify the specific problem area, identify possible resources, plan to utilize these resources, and then follow through on the plan.

Objectives

- The student will identify available resources to assist him or her in making decisions or life changes.
- The student will use given questions to map out general strategies for making decisions or life changes.

Introduction

1. Ask students to think about the following situations:

   If you were lost in a strange city, how could you find your way? *(ask a police officer, use a map, call someone you know in the city, etc.)*

   If you wanted to buy a new coat but didn't have quite enough money, how could you get the coat? *(borrow the money from a friend, work extra hours, etc.)*

   If you were tired of your job and wanted to do something different, how could you go about getting a new job? *(check the classified ads, take training for a new skill, take night courses at a local college, do volunteer work in a new setting, etc.)*

2. Explain that the students' responses involve some type of **resource**—something they can do, someone whom they can ask, some skill they can learn, etc.—that can help them out of the situation or make some sort of change.

Worksheet #39: Taking Inventory of Resources

Synopsis: By taking a personal inventory of available resources, students can begin thinking about who or what is potentially available to them in times of need or in situations that require making decisions and changes.

Directions: Students are to look over a list of suggested potential resources and to identify those that are available to them personally.

Discussion Questions:

1. Were you surprised at how many resources you could come up with?
2. Do you find you are utilizing some of these resources now?
3. Are you (or could you be) a resource person for someone else?

Worksheet #40: Changing Your Self-Esteem

Synopsis: Once a list of resources has been identified, the student can then analyze which factors involving those resources can be altered, either through time, conscious effort, or just plain luck.

Directions: Factors are listed on the worksheet, followed by three columns that indicate the likelihood of that factor being changed: can't change, can be changed (right now), or can be changed (later). Students are to put an X in the appropriate column.

Discussion Questions:

1. No one can predict for sure what factors will make a change in someone's life, but looking over the list, what are some factors that could consciously be changed by someone who is motivated to make changes? *(skills; choosing friends; being more organized; attitude; etc.)*
2. On the other hand, what are some factors that people have little control over? *(diseases; tragedies; living conditions especially as a child; etc.)*

Worksheet #41: Battle Plan

Synopsis: A list of questions (that can be utilized throughout the lessons in Part III) is presented for students to consider as they make plans to combat areas of low self-esteem.

Directions: Students are to read the list of questions presented for use in making practical plans for dealing with areas of low self-esteem. At this point, students are to think in general terms of how such changes might affect his or her self-esteem.

Lesson Review

1. List at least three personal resources or situations that can be utilized to make changes in your situation, either presently or in the future.
2. List at least three personal resources or situations that are unable or unlikely to be changed in your situation.

Journal-Entry Ideas

- Who is your most supportive or steady human resource? Why?
- When you envision yourself in a job or career, how important is the financial aspect of it? Are you in it for the money?
- What skills or talents are you currently trying to develop? How much time (per week) do you spend working on this skill?
- When was the last time you can think of that really challenged your values? What did you do? What made you feel so strongly about the situation?
- Do you consider yourself to have a good attitude? Why or why not?

Teacher Journal

Think of one specific episode in which you made a conscious, directed effort to change something about your life. What resources were involved? Did it turn out to be a permanent change? . . . for the better?

Goal for the Day

Today I will take an informal assessment of what resources I depend on as I go through the day. Maybe it will surprise me to find out what a varied support system I have developed!

Name________________________________ Date ____________

Taking Inventory of Resources

Worksheet #39

Directions: Look over the following lists of resources that may be available to you. Add your own ideas to the list. Circle the resources available to you.

Supportive People

—family member(s) ____________

—friend(s) ____________

—a best friend ____________

—school counselor ____________

—police ____________

—teacher

—religious leader

Financial Resources

—having a savings/checking account ____________

—having a job ____________

—parents willing to pay for some of your expenses ____________

____

—employable for the future ____________

Skills and Talents

—able to perform some skills well ____________

—have certificates, degrees in school, achievements ____________

____

—able to learn new things ____________

—take advantages of opportunities to improve self (community learning, volunteer experiences, etc.) ____________

Good Health

—feel well, alert, and healthy ______

—exercise regularly ______

—not preoccupied with being sick ______

—free from pain or disease ______

______

Strong Sense of Values, Purpose, Direction in Life

—have clear idea of what's important ______

—know right from wrong ______

—able to make and achieve goals ______

—want to take control of own life ______

—feel that life is good, important, and meaningful ______

Organization

—able to make and keep appointments ______

—good sense of time ______

—able to plan ahead ______

—balance work and school with leisure time ______

______

—organized in personal life (possessions, duties, work)

Attitude

—want to make positive changes ______

—have commitment to see things through ______

—can find power within self to handle difficulties ______

______

—know how and when to call upon resources ______

—have common sense

—make reality checks

—accept situations that cannot be changed

Name______________________________ Date ____________

Changing Your Self-Esteem

Worksheet #40

Directions: Which of the following factors can be changed for you? Remember that some things will change given some time, but some you must deal with right now. Put an X in the appropriate column.

	Can't Change	Can Be Changed . . . Right Now	Later
People in My Life			
1. family members			
2. my friends			
3. people I work with			
4. peers			
5. having a husband or wife			
Living Conditions			
1. where I live (town, community)			
2. with whom I live (family, siblings)			
3. having my own space (own room)			
Financial Resources			
1. how much money/income I have			
2. working a part-time job			
3. parents able/willing to help me with finances			
Skills			
1. able to do some things very well			
2. able to learn new skills			
3. willing to practice and put the time in to learn something new			
4. plan to graduate from high school			
5. able to get some skills that will help to get a job			
6. know where to look to get additional training or experience			

(Worksheet #40 continued)

	Can't Change	Can Be Changed . . . Right Now	Later
Health			
1. the condition of my health			
2. the time and effort I put into staying healthy			
3. avoiding unhealthy habits			
4. accepting my situation if I have a disability or unhealthy condition			
Values and Direction			
1. clearly can identify what is important to me			
2. know right from wrong			
3. what I know about the needs and conditions of other people			
Organization			
1. the condition of my work area			
2. the organization of my room			
3. ability to plan ahead and keep appointments			
4. turning in work or projects on time			
Attitude			
1. willing to consider new information and change my opinion			
2. know where to find resources			
3. willing to use resources			
4. willing to make changes			

Name____ Date ______________

Battle Plan

Worksheet #41

Directions: Use the following questions to think through how you might combat low self-esteem in your weak areas.

1. Who are some people who could help me in this situation?

2. What financial resources might help me?

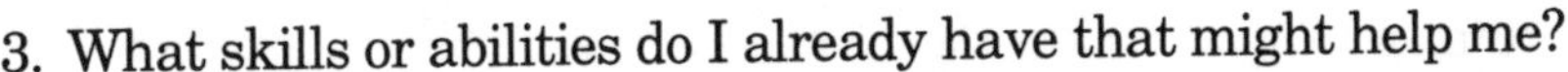

3. What skills or abilities do I already have that might help me?

4. How can I learn some new skills that might help me?

5. If I felt better, could I handle this situation better? If so, what can I do to improve how I feel physically?

6. Is there a conflict of values in this situation? What? What am I SURE about that is right, wrong, or extremely important in this situation? (What is not negotiable?)

7. Do I have the commitment to tackle this problem? Will I stick with it? Do I really intend to resolve this?

8. How can I organize my life, my time, and other resources to take care of this situation?

9. What "reality checks" can I make to ensure that I am looking at this problem objectively?

10. Do I have a good attitude about this situation? How does this show?

Lesson 21: "I don't like myself."

Examples of Behavior:

—thinks he/she is ugly, unattractive

—morose demeanor

—feels sorry for self

—sloppy, unkempt appearance

—can't accept a compliment

—makes derogatory comments about self

Reasons:

—repeatedly rejected by peers (e.g., last one picked for teams)

—compared to siblings or peers by others

—may be overweight, underweight, have health or skin problems

—may be unathletic or uncoordinated

—told by others that he/she has negative traits

—ignored by family

—unrealistic concept of what he/she should be like

Case Study:

Tommy struggled with second-grade reading material while in eighth grade. He was constantly being compared to his older brother, Mark, who was a straight-A student, good athlete, and well-liked by peers. "Why can't you do better in school?" his mother would question him. Despite being in special education classes, going to a tutor, having sessions with a professional counselor, and being under a doctor's supervision for medication, Tommy just could not be like his brother. "I guess I must be stupid," he admitted. "My brother is so good at everything. It doesn't seem like we could even be from the same family. Why is everything so hard for me? I can't even read baby stuff." His only consolation seemed to be in playing video games. He could even beat his brother at those. When life seemed awful, he could close himself up in his room and play for hours.

Things to Try:

For the student

1. Realistically assess your talents and abilities—check with others who know you!
2. Develop some talents and interests.
3. Look for school or human resources to help you, don't fight them.
4. Clean yourself up. Do what you can to make yourself clean and attractive.
5. Stop making negative self-statements; people may be tired of hearing them.
6. Start speaking positively about yourself; not bragging, but being open with others.

For the teacher

1. Don't accept negative, whiney comments; ask for rephrasing ("I'm stupid" vs. "I'm having trouble with this.").
2. Help the student find his or her talents.
3. Offer extra help on developing skills without being judgmental.
4. Help the student realize potential resources.
5. Highlight the student in class whenever possible.
6. Be sensitive to the student's weaknesses (e.g., don't have him/her read out loud in class if it is embarrassing).

For the parent

1. Accept each of your children as individuals; don't compare.
2. Praise your child for accomplishments (what he/she can do).
3. Praise your child for positive characteristics (what he/she is).
4. Give your child opportunities to "shine"; demonstrate his/her skills.
5. Give moral support.
6. Practice listening.
7. Tell about embarrassing moments you had as a child.

Activity #1: Case Study

Share the case study with students (either copy or read the paragraph to students). Using Worksheet #41, "Battle Plan," have students come up with a plan for Tommy.

Activity #2: Personal Application

If this is a problem area for the individual, have him or her work through Worksheet #41 with personal applications.

Activity #3: Worksheet #42, One Good Thing About Me

Synopsis: Students should be able to identify at least one clear-cut attribute that they realize is valuable. This "one good thing" can be highlighted by any of several means—writing, drawing, or other presentation.

Directions: Have students display in writing, drawing, or using other means, one particularly good thing about themselves.

Discussion Questions:

1. Did you have a hard time coming up with an idea? Why?
2. Did you choose something you have heard others say about you or something you know about yourself that you may not have ever shared with anyone else?
3. Did you choose to depict something you did, something you plan to do, something you are, or something you hope to be?

Journal-Entry Ideas

- There may be something wonderful about yourself that you are hiding from others or that you feel protective about. Why do you feel you can't share this with others?
- What specifically don't you like about yourself? Is it something you can change?
- What negative comments do you find yourself making about yourself? What could you substitute for these comments?

Name________________________________ Date ______________

One Good Thing About Me

Worksheet #42

Directions: Draw a picture, write a paragraph, use whatever means you want to express yourself, but show ONE THING about yourself that you are really proud of.

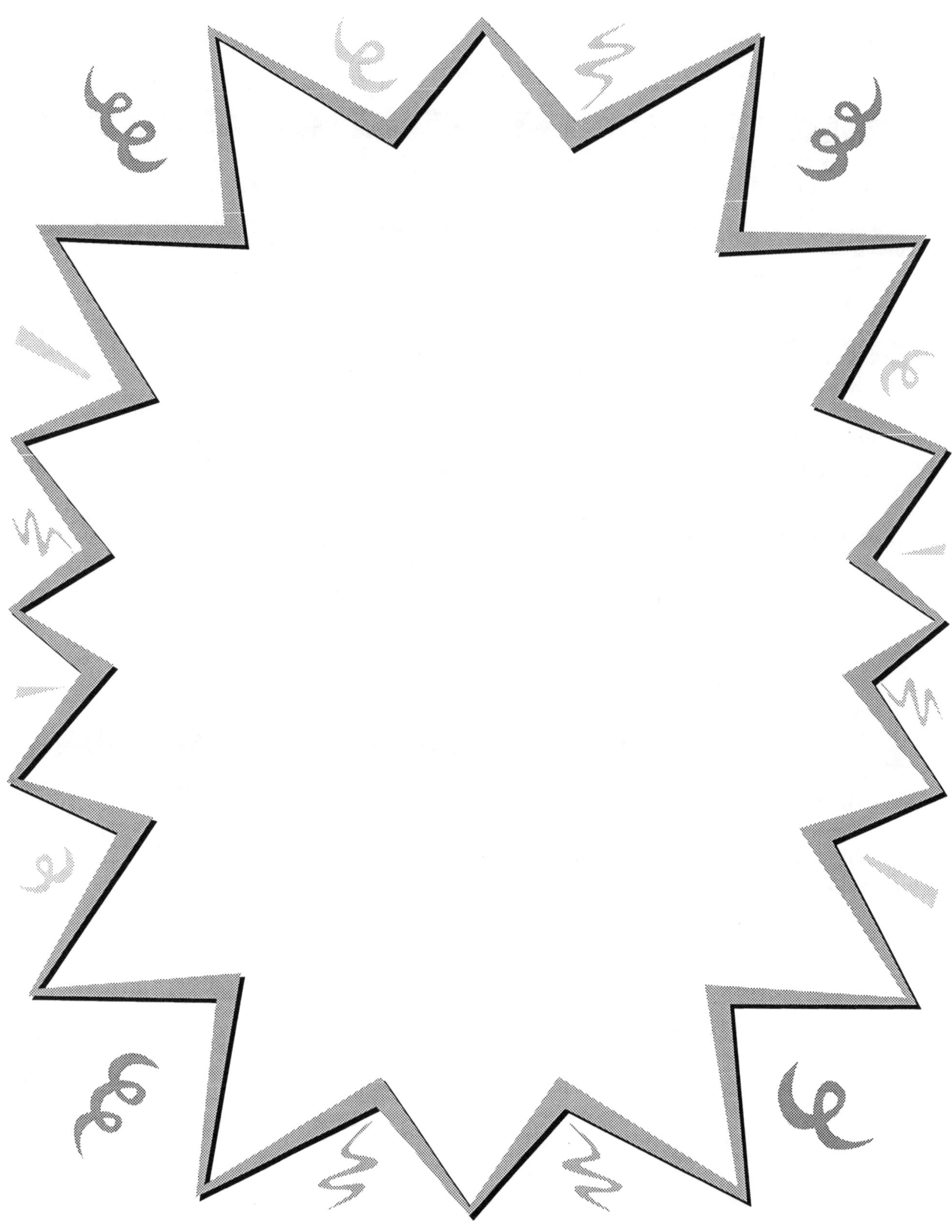

Lesson 22: "Nothing ever goes right for me."

Examples of Behavior:

—pessimistic attitude

—low expectations of self and others

—won't attempt new tasks ("too hard")

—afraid to make mistakes

—often fails in school

—low self-confidence

—won't make commitment to follow through on tasks; allows failure without trying to prevent it

Reasons:

—poor academic skills

—poor social skills

—has been ridiculed in past for mistakes

—nervous, uptight attitude

—has had past encounters with failure

—not held accountable for outcome of tasks

—low energy

—poor work habits

Case Study:

Rajid had had several part-time jobs after school and during summers, but they never lasted long. Usually it was only a matter of days until he would get fired—for poor attendance, being rude to a customer, or doing an inadequate job. Rajid's comments: "The boss doesn't like me. No one ever explains what I'm supposed to do. No rude customer is going to talk to me like that! It's a rotten job anyway, I'll look for something else."

Things to Try:

For the student

1. Make small goals and stick with them.
2. Get someone to help you stay on task (check in with a friend).
3. Be realistic about your attitude.
4. Put the past behind you; today is a new day.
5. Make sure you understand what is expected of you on tasks (school, job, home).
6. Ask questions if you aren't sure what to do.
7. Ask for responsibility.
8. Plan ahead—what is everything that could go wrong? what will I do if that happens?
9. Assess your situation—are you in over your head?

For the teacher

1. Make realistic requirements for the student.
2. Be sure your directions/explanations are clear and are understood by the student.
3. Don't bring up past student failure experiences.
4. Praise student for taking a risk.

5. Allow student to assist in formulating classroom goals.
6. Make extra study guides and resources readily available for student.

For the parent

1. Don't expect your child to fail; be a good model.
2. Offer to help child at home with difficult tasks.
3. Be a resource for your child.
4. Don't "buy in" to whining; offer to listen to sincere feelings being expressed.

Activity #1: Case Study

Have students read/listen to the case study. Using Worksheet #41, "Battle Plan," have students brainstorm for ideas to help Rajid.

Activity #2: Personal Application

Have students work through Worksheet #41 using personal resources if this is a problem area.

Activity #3: Worksheet #43, Make It Happen, Make It Right

Synopsis: Students are given the opportunity to select one task and ensure success of that task by overpreparing—making sure that all bases are covered, anything that can go wrong will be considered, and then making the commitment to follow through on carrying out the task.

Directions: Students are to consider the two examples of tasks that were successfully completed by overpreparing. They are then to select a personal task to undertake and plan how they will successfully carry it out.

Discussion Questions:

1. What type of task did you select—academic, social, physical, etc.?
2. What was your method of making sure you would be successful?
3. Are there other methods you could have tried? What?
4. How does it feel to be successful? Was it worth the effort?
5. If you are successful once on a task, do you think you would be more likely to try it again?

Journal-Entry Ideas

- What is something you avoid because you assume you will fail? What makes this so difficult for you?
- Does worrying about what might go wrong do any good? Why do people worry anyway?
- Have you ever had a day in which everything seemed to go wrong? Tell about it.
- What things have happened to you as a result of just plain "bad luck"? What about "good luck"?

Name______________________________ Date ____________

Make It Happen, Make It Right

Worksheet #43

Directions: Make something go right by overpreparing. Choose a task (examples below) and decide how you will overprepare for the task. Carry it out—do it right—enjoy the success!

Task #1: Spelling Test
Normally I spend about 30 seconds looking over my words. I get a B or C. But this time, I'm going for 100%.
First, I'm going to make sure I know which words will be on the test. I've got them all copied here.
SPELLING WORDS
I'm going to copy them a couple of times . . .
Then have my brother call them to me every night until I KNOW I'll get them right. I am 100% confident that I KNOW them!
Test time—no problem. I'll sail through this easily.
100%
100%
Task #2: Cleaning Your Bedroom
I hate this job. But this time I'm going to make sure it exceeds my mom's expectations.
Vacuum . . . dust . . . change the sheets . . . spray the windows . . .
Books here . . . dirty clothes there . . . what is this? Throw it out, I guess.
There! When my mom takes a look in here, she'll think she's in the wrong house!

Lesson 23: "I can't change anything, so why try?"

Examples of Behavior:

—passive; doesn't even try to argue

—rarely does homework

—accepts injustices without fighting back

—blames others for his/her failures

—apathetic towards most things

—lets others make decisions for him/her

—sloppy or careless work

Reasons:

—doesn't see practical applications

—past encounters with failing

—unrealistic about abilities (underestimates self)

—dominant parents or siblings

—put down by others

Case Study:

Belinda was in eighth grade for the second time. Usually she started out each school year with the attitude that she was going to do better, but by the first grading period the pattern was the same: missed assignments, frequent absences, and lack of interest with anything to do with school. Her mother reported that she had little control over what Belinda did after school; she was often out with friends until late hours of the evening. Belinda used her passivity to get teachers to say: "You're never going to make it," then used that statement as an excuse. "Well, I'm never going to make it—you just told me that. So why should I try?"

Things to Try:

For the student

1. Decide whether or not changes are possible in situations.
2. Examine all possible resources for change.
3. Think through how you **do** affect others.
4. Determine long-range consequences for passive behavior.

For the teacher

1. Encourage student to make decisions.
2. Teach student to view small successes as important.
3. Give student responsibility.
4. Don't overreact to student's passivity.
5. Teach consequences of behavior.
6. Set realistic standards for work and don't accept less.

For the parent

1. Don't do too much for your child; teach responsibility for actions and tasks.
2. Praise child for making decisions.

3. Don't try to get a reaction (this may backfire).
4. Model assertive behavior.
5. Don't be drawn into no-win arguments.

Activity #1: Case Study

Discuss the case study with students. Using Worksheet #41, "Battle Plan," have students come up with ideas to help Belinda become more assertive.

Activity #2: Personal Application

If the student needs to become assertive, use Worksheet #41 to have him or her come up with a personal plan.

Activity #3: Worksheet #44, Exercise in POWER!

Synopsis: Students can experience the feeling of power by making changes. That change may be the accomplishment of a small task or going above and beyond a requirement. Students are to make changes in their lives (or someone else's) by specifically carrying out a chosen task.

Directions: Students are to choose a task (suggestions are given on the worksheet) and to carry it out.

Discussion Questions:

1. Did you make a change in your or someone else's life by completing your task? How?
2. What reaction did you get from someone after (or while) completing the task?
3. Did you feel more powerful by completing this task?

Journal-Entry Ideas

- Who is the most powerful person you can think of? Where does he or she get his or her power or authority?
- Who is the most powerful person in your life? Why do you feel this person is powerful? What influence does he/she have over you?

Name____ Date ______________

Exercise in POWER!

Worksheet #44

Directions: Decide to do something to make an immediate positive change in your life—or someone else's. Read the list of suggestions below and add your own. Then circle the one you are going to do. Follow through!

Ideas

—clean up a yard

—do an extra-credit report

—make a cup of coffee for your parent

—babysit for free

—wash all of the dishes in the sink

—write a letter to a relative

—visit someone in the hospital

—clean out the garage

—buy some flowers for your mother or aunt

—turn in a perfect math paper

—join a school recycling club

____

____

____

____

____

____

____

____

____

____

____

Lesson 24: "I don't get along with others."

Examples of Behavior:

—provokes others
—defensive attitude
—sets up other people to react negatively
—has to have the last word
—avoids others
—puts self in problem situations
—usually the scapegoat
—bullied by others
—teases others
—last one picked for teams

Reasons:

—poor social skills
—impulsive (acts first, thinks later)
—bad experiences with others
—thinks of himself or herself as superior/inferior to others
—not able to "read" others' behavior accurately (misinterprets)
—looks/acts very differently from peer group

Case Study:

Carl gets along with adults and children, but does not relate well at all to people his own age. He doesn't feel he has any common interests with them. In the past, he has gotten into fights at school with students who have made fun of him (he is overweight and a poor student). Carl hates working in groups at school and avoids sports, clubs, and other situations that involve being with others. He would rather be alone than have to get along with people he doesn't like—which is mostly everyone.

Things to Try:

For the student

1. Concentrate on making one good friend.
2. Join a group or club with common interests; focus on the activity rather than other people at first.
3. Decide ahead of time what your course of action will be in conflict situations.
4. Look for opportunities to share your interests with others who may be interested in what you do.
5. Look for good points in other people.
6. Practice doing kind things for other people.

For the teacher

1. Pair student with easy-going, likeable students for class activities.
2. Look for opportunities to highlight the student in class.
3. Make classroom/school rules clear to all students; be an impartial judge in conflicts.

For the parent

1. Encourage child to join interest groups/activities.
2. Make it easy for your child to invite friends over for safe, appropriate activities.
3. Ask for both sides of a story/conflict; try to get your child to be impartial when relating "what happened."
4. Some students are "loners" and may not require a lot of social interaction; but be sure your child is involved in some healthy pursuits.

Activity #1: Case Study

Read or write and copy the case study for students. Have them go through Worksheet #41, "Battle Plan," to make a plan for Carl.

Activity #2: Personal Application

If this is a problem area for the child, have him or her work through Worksheet #41 with personal applications.

Activity #3: Worksheet #45, Problem People

Synopsis: Certain types of people can "push your buttons" and cause you to react. Several examples of unlikeable people are given for students to consider.

Directions: Have students complete the worksheet by circling the characters with whom they would have trouble getting along.

Discussion Questions:

1. Which personality types are particularly annoying to you? Why?
2. How would you handle each of the situations on the worksheet?
3. Have you ever been in similar situations? What happened?

Journal-Entry Ideas

- Who are the people who are the most difficult for you to get along with? Why do you feel this way?
- Have you ever had an experience in which someone you didn't like became a friend? What happened to make this change?
- Do you feel you have personality characteristics that others find unappealing? Who has told you about these? What do you think?

Name____ Date ______________

Problem People

Worksheet #45

Directions: Which of the following people would you have trouble getting along with? Circle them and tell why.

---

1. Insulting Iggy

Boy, you look stupid today!

---

2. Athletic Al

Do you have to be on our team? Why are we so lucky?

---

3. Cocky Calla

I never have any trouble with math—it's so easy for me. I don't know why you're having problems!

---

4. Teasing Terri

Whooo - look who got new shoes!

---

5. Volatile Victor

Wanna fight? Come on - let's go outside and settle this!

Lesson 25: "I am afraid of changes."

We have a strange and wonderful attachment to each other.

Examples of Behavior:

—anxious; anticipates events

—sleeplessness

—worries about things that may not happen

—wants to do things the "old" way

—dependent on familiar people

—resorts to immature behavior for attention

—certain that things will go wrong

Reasons:

—does not clearly understand his/her present situation

—unable to predict likely consequences

—does not have enough information about the changes

—is very comfortable in present situation

—has weak support system (few friends, apathetic parents)

—disorganized; life is unstructured and chaotic

Case Study:

Angela began worrying about the start of a new school year almost before summer vacation started. She was sure her new teachers wouldn't like her, she would fail, she would get lost in a new building, and she wouldn't be able to understand work that was a grade harder. To make things worse, her family was moving to a new house over the summer. Angela was depressed about that, worrying that she wouldn't make new friends, her things would be lost in the move, and fearful of getting lost while trying to find places from a new starting point. During the nights she would toss and turn, worrying ahead of time of everything that would go wrong.

Things to Try:

For the student

1. Find out as much as you can about the conditions your change will bring.
2. Prepare yourself as much as possible; think through possible events and outcomes.
3. Talk to a friend or someone who will listen to you.
4. Find someone to talk to who may have been through a similar problem.
5. Write down your fears (specifically); set your paper aside and look at it later when you may be more calm.

For the teacher

1. Refer student to the school counselor if appropriate.
2. Emphasize the teaching of study skills (especially to poor students who worry about school-related difficulties).
3. Emphasize positive outcomes of new events/situations.
4. Prevent problems by having student tour new building, meet new teachers, explain new systems or procedures.
5. Remind student of past successes when challenges were met.

For the parent

1. Take time to explain upcoming changes (move, divorce, illness in family) to your child.
2. Model a positive attitude or outlook.

3. If fears are unrealistic, try logic and common sense.
4. If fears are excessive, you may need to consider professional help from a counselor or therapist.
5. Realize that some people take longer to adapt to changes than others; give the situation a reasonable length of time to work out.

ACTIVITY #1: CASE STUDY

Have students discuss the case study using Worksheet #41, "Battle Plan," to guide students through making suggestions for Angela.

ACTIVITY #2: PERSONAL APPLICATION

Have students work through Worksheet #41 if this is a problem for individual students.

ACTIVITY #3: WORKSHEET #46, LEAVING THE PLANET

Synopsis: Students are given the opportunity to work through a hypothetical situation in which they are leaving the planet to live in a new society. Many changes, of course, are involved in this, and students must consider how best to prepare for them.

Directions: Students are to review information necessary for making plans to move to a new planet. Students can prepare their own ideas or set up situations for other students to solve.

Discussion Questions:

1. Why do you think some people enjoy changes? What types of people or occupations involve a lot of change?
2. Some changes are perceived as good, others as bad. Are there changes that are simply DIFFERENT?
3. What do you think are the best defenses for handling changes?

JOURNAL-ENTRY IDEAS

- What is an example of a major change in your life? Was this a positive, negative, or neutral change? How has it affected the way you are today?
- How do you handle fear of the unknown?

Name________________________________ Date ____________

Leaving the Planet

Worksheet #46

Directions: Pretend you are going through a very major change—you're leaving the planet to move to a new society. It is not your choice; it is necessary for your survival. Think about what questions you will need to ask and answer regarding the move and settling in. What will you need to anticipate? Make thorough preparations. (1) Complete the following information in a general manner. (2) Set up limits for someone else to complete and exchange papers!

1. What the living conditions are like there (language, food, society):

____

____

2. How you will make the move (getting yourself transported, time involved):

____

____

3. What you will need to take to survive:

____

____

4. People and things to take along (how much room is available, restrictions on other people):

____

____

5. Dangers to anticipate (source of information):

____

____

6. Good things to anticipate: ______________________________

____

7. Things to take for pleasure and enjoyment:

____

____

8. What you will do the first day, first week, first month:

____

____

Lesson 26: "No one else feels like I do."

Examples of Behavior:

—often withdrawn; isolates self from others

—complains that no one understands him/her

—sets self apart from others

—may exaggerate handicap ("I can't do that because I have a learning disability.")

—won't reach out to others or accept offers of help

—does not trust others

—has few friends, little sociability

Reasons:

—may look or act substantially different from peers

—parents gave child attention for having a handicap, being "different"

—may have had a traumatic experience and isn't sure how to sort through it

—wants attention through negative comments about self

—extremely introspective

—thinks of self as superior or inferior to others

Case Study:

Stephan has a learning disability. It is mild, but he still attends a resource room for a period of time each day at school. Other students don't make fun of him, but Stephan has decided that he is not well-liked because he is different. His grades are average, he is a reasonably good athlete, and he has a good sense of humor when he wants to share that with others. However, most of the time he prefers to be alone. At home, he does not want to talk to his parents about any problems since he thinks they won't understand him anyway. "Why should I bother talking to anyone about how I feel?" he asks. "No one is me; no one knows what I'm going through or what I feel. They say they do, but they don't."

Things to Try:

For the student

1. Make an effort to be more open with selected people.
2. Turn your thoughts outward instead of inward; see things through the eyes of other people.
3. Try to explain how you feel to others; you may find that someone shares your experiences.
4. Get involved in a group project (community recycling, neighborhood repairs, etc.); become part of a team.
5. If you have a diagnosed handicap, find out about it—not just the limits, but the possibilities.

For the teacher

1. Give students the opportunity to voice opinions without judgment.
2. Use videos that focus on teen problems in the classroom; include discussion.

3. Many students go through "moody" periods; explain that within limits this is normal for everyone.
4. Relate anecdotes from your own life to students.
5. Invite speakers to your class who have overcome a handicap.
6. Choose reading selections that are appropriate and focus on teen challenges.

For the parent

1. Encourage your child to join a healthy group (church youth group, scouting, community groups).
2. Make it easy for your child to talk to you; be accessible, listen without commenting, share an activity.
3. Reassure your child that feeling isolated is common to everyone.
4. Stress ways that he/she is similar to other members of your family. (Did a relative have a similar problem?)
5. Let child know that differences can be uniqueness; depends on point of view.

Activity #1: Case Study

Use Worksheet #41, "Battle Plan," to have students think through suggestions for Stephan.

Activity #2: Personal Application

If feelings of being alone are a problem for the student, have him or her work through Worksheet #41 to make plans for change.

Activity #3: Worksheet #47, Biography

Synopsis: Students may find a "link" with another person by reading a biography (or autobiography) of someone who is of interest to them.

Directions: Students should select an individual, read a biography (or autobiography) of that person, and answer discussion questions about that person's life and experiences.

Journal-Entry Ideas

- What sets you apart from others? What is it about you that is different from anyone else?
- No one understands how I feel about . . .

Name____ Date ______________

Biography

Worksheet #47

Directions: Read a short biography (or autobiography) of a person who interests you. This could be someone presently living or someone who has done something in the past that is noteworthy. Find or copy a picture of the person to display. Answer the following questions.

1. Why did you select this person?

____

____

____

2. What did this person do that was interesting?

____

____

____

3. What problems did this person encounter?

____

____

____

4. What do you admire about this person?

____

____

____

5. What do you think you and this person might have in common?

____

____

____

____

____

____

Lesson 27: "I am not important."

Examples of Behavior:

—extremely quiet

—does not volunteer for tasks

—withdraws from groups

—puts self down constantly

—low energy level

—does not take care of personal appearance

—passive attitude

—will do something dramatic (usually unhealthy) for attention

Reasons:

—has had comments or opinions ridiculed by others

—expends energy on tasks, but sees no changes

—is overlooked in groups

—rarely praised by adults

—not accepted by peer group

Case Study:

Janelle's first memory of school was in kindergarten, when she was the only one in the class to not get a sticker on a coloring paper. The teacher had simply overlooked her, and didn't even know there was a problem until she found Janelle crying in the back of the room. One of four children, Janelle felt loved by her parents, but did not receive a lot of individual attention from either one. She did not make friends easily, and when others had already formed their groups, she was often left out. The students in her class didn't particularly want to isolate her; they just didn't notice her. She wasn't outstanding in any special way they could see. In time, she stopped raising her hand to answer questions in class, brought books to read instead of joining in with others at recess, and in later years, kept her opinions to herself for fear that they weren't what the teachers were looking for.

Things to Try:

For the student

1. Make a *conscious effort* to participate in class each day (raise hand, talk to another student, ask a question).
2. Wear something you would not normally wear; use the attention to strike up a conversation with others.
3. Ask your parents for responsibility in some way.
4. Offer to do needed jobs; give yourself a role.
5. Decide to make yourself important to one person; adopt an elderly person in a nursing home, become a "big brother" or "big sister."
6. Work on developing a talent or skill that you enjoy; get better at it!

For the teacher

1. Use cooperative learning techniques in the classroom; group projects.
2. Seat the student in the front of the room.
3. Ask the student for his/her opinion in discussions.

4. Speak to the student individually; inquire about interests.
5. Pay attention (use eye contact) when the student speaks.

For the parent

1. Arrange to spend time individually with your child.
2. Display certificates earned, trophies, good papers, etc.
3. Give child jobs to do, then remember to praise the outcome.
4. Assign a specific task to your child for which he/she is responsible; remind him/her of the importance of it.
5. Ask your child for suggestions/opinions about family situations.
6. Praise your child honestly in front of others.

ACTIVITY #1: CASE STUDY

Use Worksheet #41, "Battle Plan," to have students work through possible solutions for Janelle's feelings of being unimportant.

ACTIVITY #2: PERSONAL APPLICATION

Have students complete questions on Worksheet #41 if this is a problem area.

ACTIVITY #3: WORKSHEET #48, INVISIBLE FOR A DAY

Synopsis: Students who feel they are unimportant may feel "invisible," as though no one notices them. By thinking about what life would be like without them, they may realize their importance to others.

Directions: Students are to think through what a day would be like if they were invisible to other people. They are to write down their thoughts about how situations and people would be influenced without them.

Discussion Questions:

1. Who would be most affected by your absence? Why?
2. What events would be affected by your absence? How?
3. Who or what would you feel badly about missing if you were invisible?

JOURNAL-ENTRY IDEAS

- What type(s) of reactions would you hope to get from other people if you were suddenly gone? Why?
- Who would you most like to eavesdrop on if you were invisible?
- How do you feel when you are suddenly given a lot of attention (for something you did well!)? Does this embarrass you, especially if it is in front of your friends? How would you prefer to be given attention if you did something important?

Name____ Date ______________

Invisible for a Day

Worksheet #48

Directions: What would life be like without you? Go through a day (choose which day you want) and write about what would happen if you were invisible—but able to see, hear, and feel what was going on. You are unable to communicate with anyone. Use the ideas below to get you started.

What would life be like . . .

in the morning, getting up around your house

at school or work

with your friends

jobs that wouldn't get done

people who would miss you

what people would say about you

____

____

____

____

____

____

____

____

____

____

____

____

____

____

____

____

____

____

____

Lesson 28: "Everything is always my fault."

Examples of Behavior:

—reputation for getting into trouble

—tends to be where problems arise

—gets caught when does something wrong

—picked on by others

—blamed for things based on hearsay, reputation

—provides a reaction when blamed by others

—has little confidence in worth of opinions, answers

—expects to be blamed for things

Reasons:

—an "easy target" for others

—the weakest party in relationships (youngest child, submissive to peers, easy to pick on)

—may have an undeserved reputation based on past mistakes (or even peer/family associations)

—careless, disorganized, leaves self open for making mistakes

—uses poor judgment, falls into traps

Case Study:

Roy had a reputation for being a trouble-maker starting in kindergarten. He was the kid who was always tearing up things in the boys' restroom, getting other kids to laugh out loud in class, and starting fights among others. Although Roy was generally a friendly, likeable kid, he was the first one targeted by teachers, parents in the neighborhood, and eventually the police when things went wrong. Unfortunately, he admitted to being involved in some vandalism (stealing CBs out of cars), and hung around with other kids who already had juvenile records. One day he came to school with a chain around his neck and a hood ornament from an expensive car hanging from it. He insisted he didn't break it off a car; it was given to him by one of his friends. "But I might as well say that I stole it," he said, bitterly. "No one believes me anyway."

Things to Try:

For the student

1. Try to see yourself through the eyes of others; what sort of reputation do you have?
2. Are you being blamed for things you **are** responsible for? Is this unfair? Try to assess the situation objectively.
3. Get a clear idea of what is expected of you when you are given a task to do.
4. Get a clear idea of who is responsible for doing what when several people are involved in tasks.
5. Realize that some things are beyond your control; you are not responsible or to blame for outcomes.

For the teacher

1. Be careful of assigning blame to specific students if you are unsure of their role in a matter.
2. Don't use past reputations to color your feelings of students; give each one a clean slate.
3. Discuss with students the importance of having a good reputation.

4. Students may judge themselves more harshly than others; use peer courts to practice sorting through situations.

For the parent

1. Are you being consistent and objective when blaming your child? Do you have all the facts?
2. Make sure you aren't taking out frustrations from your own work or problems on your child; take time out for yourself if you need to.
3. Praise your child for "owning up" to taking responsibility if something is his/her fault.

Activity #1: Case Study

Have students offer suggestions for helping Roy with his problem of being blamed for something he didn't do by using Worksheet #41, "Battle Plan."

Activity #2: Personal Application

If this is a problem area for students, have them use Worksheet #41 to make a plan.

Activity #3: Worksheet #49, The Blame Game

Synopsis: By thinking through situations in which others may or may not be responsible for something going wrong, students can learn to be objective, look for clues, and practice exercising good judgment.

Directions: Students are to write and perform short role-plays or skits using the ideas on the worksheet. Each of the ideas involves someone being blamed for something.

Discussion Questions:

1. Is it always important to blame someone, to find out who is responsible for something going wrong? Is it OK to just let some things go?
2. How important is having a good reputation when you are in a situation in which things look bad for you? Will this "save" you?
3. Can you think of examples of situations in which it looked as though someone was responsible for something, but he/she turned out to be totally innocent? Has this ever happened to you?

Journal-Entry Ideas

- Have you ever been blamed for something you didn't do? What happened? Were you able to prove your innocence? How did it make you feel?
- What kind of reputation do you think you have among your friends, family, school, peers, etc.? Is this reputation deserved?
- Think about the last five events that have happened in your life that have upset you. Make two columns: my fault/not my fault. Which events should go under which column? What, if anything, can you do about the outcome of each event now?

Name______________________________ Date ______________

The Blame Game

Worksheet #49

Directions: Get a partner or form a small group. Write, direct, and perform a short play or skit using one of the following ideas:

(a) A wallet is left in a classroom. When the owner realizes it is missing and returns to the room, it is gone. Three people were known to be in the room at the time. One of them has a reputation of shoplifting. All three have denied taking or even seeing the wallet. How can you figure out "The Mystery of the Missing Wallet"?

(b) You just found out that someone has been spreading bad rumors about you. Someone whom you do not know well says that it is your best friend. This doesn't seem right, but the information being spread around is about something that only you and your very close friends know about. How will you handle this?

(c) Go through an incredibly bad day (beginning with burnt toast and ending with a bed that collapses). Who could you blame for each and every thing that goes wrong? (the dog, the weatherman, the furniture manufacturing company, etc.)

(d) You borrow a very expensive sweatshirt from a friend. Somehow pizza gets spilled on it and your friend is extremely upset. You insist that accidents happen and it's not your fault; he/she thinks you weren't being careful. What will you do?

Lesson 29: "My feelings are always getting hurt."

Examples of Behavior:

—overly sensitive to criticism

—takes self very seriously

—cries inappropriately

—demanding upon friends

—needs a lot of attention

—misjudges others (e.g., their intentions, comments)

Reasons:

—misinterprets social situations

—does not "read" others' emotions or expressions well

—does not share how he/she feels with others; keeps them guessing

—enjoys feeling sorry for self

—introspective; centers on self rather than others

Case Study:

Darcy considered Beth to be her closest, and practically only, friend. She counted on Beth to save her a seat at the lunch table and to walk around the halls together before and after school. One day Beth decided to try out for the school play—and made it. Suddenly Beth's free time was spent in rehearsals . . . and cast parties. When Darcy complained about Beth never having time to spend with her anymore, Beth said that it was a lot of fun being involved in the play and Darcy should have tried out if she wanted to meet some new people. Darcy replied that she wasn't interested in being in a play. Beth countered with informing Darcy that she should be more outgoing and realize that it's fun to get to know other people and have other interests. Darcy left, ran home, and cried. "I feel as though my only friend betrayed me," she sobbed. "We used to be best friends, now I feel left behind. I'm not fun, I'm not interesting; I guess I'm going to be alone the rest of my life."

Things to Try:

For the student

1. When upset, give yourself some time to think and let things settle.
2. Decide what reaction you want to portray when involved in emotional situations; rehearse your reaction.
3. Talk things over with a good friend who will give honest feedback.
4. Consider the source: Is the person who is offending or hurting you someone who really matters to you? Does the opinion matter?
5. Find appropriate outlets for your feelings (perhaps crying works best for you).
6. Make sure you are not misunderstanding a situation or person; ask for clarification from the person.

For the teacher

1. Be aware of sensitive students; don't overdo the criticism.
2. Find positive ways to convey something that needs to be changed or redone.
3. Sometimes a student needs to "toughen up"; state this clearly and matter-of-factly (life won't always be easy or people always friendly).
4. Notice when a student improves in this area; comment that "I noticed you handled that situation very well," etc.

For the parent

1. Help your child prepare for emotional situations in advance.
2. Model good control of emotions.
3. Encourage your child to talk things through, express feelings.
4. Realize that sometimes feelings will change over time; perhaps this is not a crisis.
5. Help your child learn from difficult situations with people by helping him/her think of ways to counter in a positive way (return good for evil).

Activity #1: Case Study

Use Worksheet #41, "Battle Plan," to have students make a plan for Darcy and her hurt feelings.

Activity #2: Personal Application

Have students work through Worksheet #41 if this is a problem area for them.

Activity #3: Worksheet #50, Riding the Emotional Roller Coaster

Synopsis: Students can probably identify specific events, people, situations, or even words that will bring on certain emotions. It is important to be aware of what can trigger certain emotions.

Directions:

Students are to complete the worksheet by filling in specific things that make them feel various emotions.

Discussion Questions:

1. How do you avoid certain situations that will make you feel uncomfortable?
2. What do you do to help yourself over life's "bumps"?
3. Have your reactions to certain people or events changed at all over the past few months or years? Do things that used to make you angry when you were younger (or less skilled or less popular or busier) still affect you the same way?
4. What are some events that trigger the same emotion in most people? (What would anger/surprise/offend most people? Are we really all that different?)

Journal-Entry Ideas

- How do you typically react when your feelings are hurt? Are you quiet and withdrawn? Do you retaliate with anger? Will you think about, stew about it, and get angry later? Explain.
- Have you ever had a day (or specified period of time) in which your emotions went from rock bottom to up in the clouds (or vice versa)? Tell about what happened.

Name____ Date ______________

Riding the Emotional Roller Coaster

Worksheet #50

Directions: Think about what makes you happy, angry, sad, distressed, silly, and so on. Complete examples of situations, people, or events that might trigger these emotions.

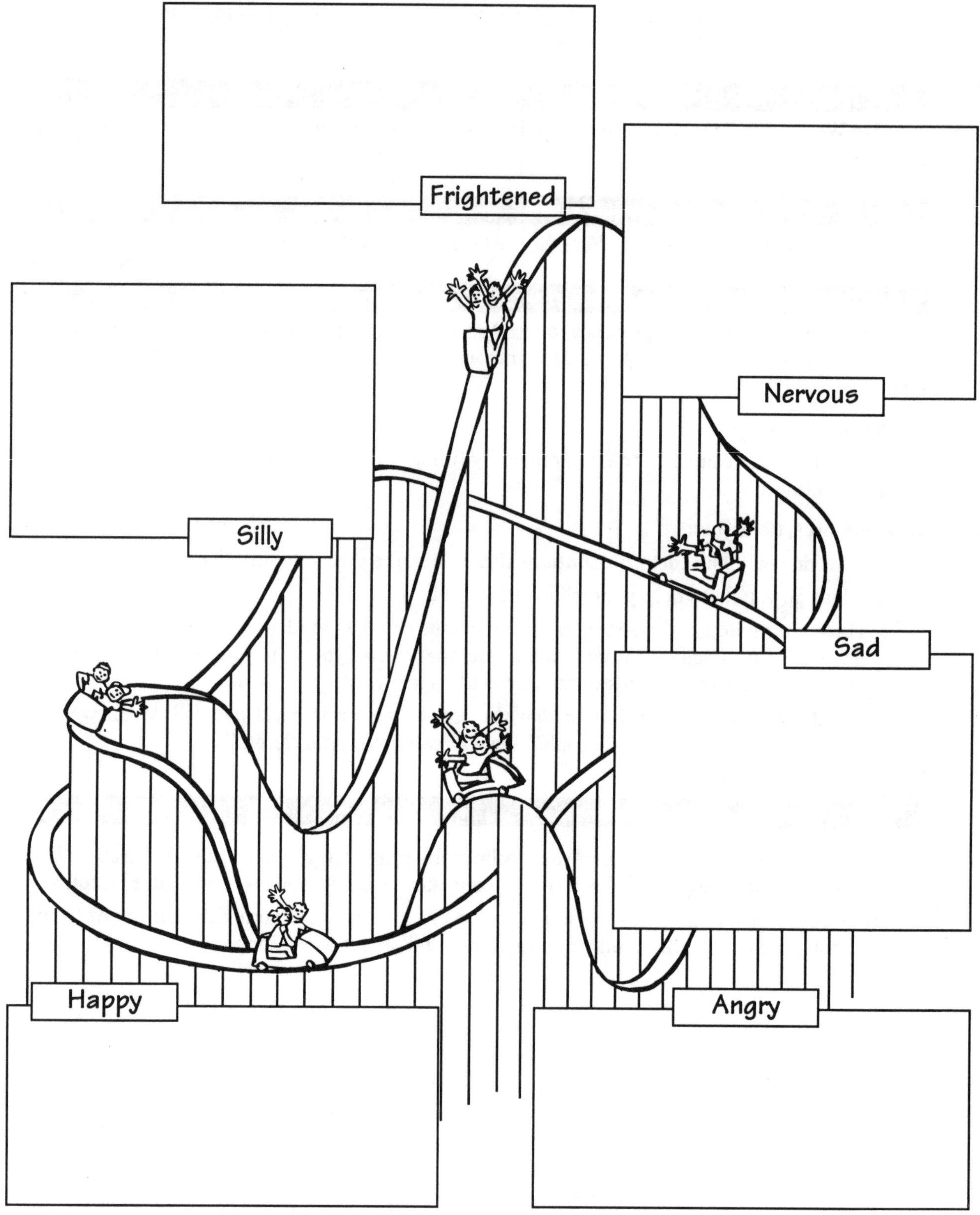

Lesson 30: "I'm never good enough; someone is always better."

Examples of Behavior:

—gets discouraged in competition

—gives up before completing tasks

—measures self against unrealistic standards

—does not give 100% effort

—feels he/she is judged unfairly

—puts pressure on self to do better

—does not recognize value of what he/she does (or produces)

Reasons:

—compared to siblings or other students

—work and actions are criticized

—does not work up to ability

—told that he/she should be doing better, but may be unable to perform better

—given unrealistic values or standards

Case Study:

Jackson enjoyed playing the trumpet in the school band. He practiced daily, took private lessons, and enjoyed playing in the various band performances. As he became older, he finally made it to be the second chair: only one person, Ted, was better than he was. Jackson was happy to be second trumpet, but his father (who had no musical ability whatsoever) insisted he should be first. "If you would only try harder, you could be first chair," he told Jackson. "When I was your age, I was on the first string in basketball. I never settled for second best. Your only goal should be getting to the top." Jackson's comments: "I play in the band because I enjoy it. Or, I used to enjoy it. Dad doesn't know anything about music or playing in the band; all he remembers is being a good athlete. That came easy to him. I'm not sure I even want the pressure of being first trumpet. I'd be afraid the person in the second chair would be waiting for me to mess up."

Things to Try:

For the student

1. Make goals. What do you want to achieve?
2. Be realistic. Is this goal attainable?
3. "Own" your goals. Do you want this for yourself or because someone else wants this for you?
4. Study the person who you feel is "better" than you at your goal. What tips can you pick up?
5. Realize that you might have to be satisfied with your best effort.

For the teacher

1. Show students how to set realistic goals.
2. Caution students of the dangers of comparing self to someone else (may not be a possibility or even desirable!).
3. Decide when to praise **effort**, and when to praise **mastery**.
4. Point out skills and training available to help students.
5. Provide drills or activities in which students compete only against themselves.
6. Use student for peer tutoring in an area in which he/she is very competent.

For the parent

1. Avoid comparing your child to unrealistic models.
2. Realize that you might (both) have to be satisfied with a good effort. Not everyone has the ability to be a star at something they're interested in.
3. Try to find measurable standards for discussing performance (define "good enough").
4. Praise small successes.
5. Emphasize skills that your child is good at.

Activity #1: Case Study

Have students use Worksheet #41, "Battle Plan," to help make a plan for Jackson to come to terms with his situation.

Activity #2: Personal Application

If students need to focus on this problem, direct them to use Worksheet #41 to make personal plans.

Activity #3: Worksheet #51, Making "Good" Better

Synopsis: Students may accept "adequate" or "good" as good enough, when there are things that they could work on to make improvements. These areas include athletics, academics, completing assigned tasks, and interest areas.

Directions: Students are to read the worksheet's examples of people who are adequate at their quest, but would like to be better. Students are then to think of ideas that would help the people improve themselves.

Discussion Questions:

1. If someone does not have the talent or ability to be the best, should they settle for being second best? Should they change activities to find something at which they can excel?
2. Are there some activities anyone could do well if they put more time and effort into it? *(activities which do not depend on having skills and talents)*
3. Who or what are some standards or authorities that are trustworthy; that is, would be good references to let someone know that what they did was "good enough"? *(a professional in the area, someone with a lot of experience, a written resource, etc.)*

Journal-Entry Ideas

- When has someone told you: "You should be doing better; that isn't good enough"? What were the circumstances? How did you feel? Did you agree or disagree?
- What is something you care a lot about, enough to put a lot of effort into? Something that even though others may think of this as hard work, you don't mind at all because you enjoy doing it or training for it.
- Pretend you are entered in a race. The winner will receive $1,000,000. What are you going to do to start training for the race? What are you going to do the night before the race? What will you be telling yourself as you are running the race? What will you do when the finish line is coming up and there is one person ahead of you?

Name________________________________ Date ______________

Making "Good" Better

Worksheet #51

Directions: What could each of the following individuals do to become better at their concern?

1. Tomas

I'm the second string quarterback on the football team. I'd sure like to get to play more by being first!

2. Amy

I got a C+ on this research paper, but my teacher said we have the whole weekend to redo our work and turn it in again on Monday.

3. Fred

This car was really a mess. I hosed it down and cleaned out some of the trash in the back seat. I think it looks better.

4. Donna

Here's my picture that I'm going to enter in the contest. Sure hope I win!

5. Ricardo

Five people are going to be picked for the parts in the play. I guess I'll have time to read the script tomorrow. Or maybe the next day. Sure hope I get the lead!

Lesson 31: "I have to be perfect."

Examples of Behavior:

—tears up work that has a mistake, and redoes it
—becomes frustrated with small imperfections
—has unrealistic standards for self
—constantly compares self to others
—looks down at others (who are not perfect)
—does not complete tasks; loses sense of time
—does not recognize when a task/project is completed
—perseveres on details; does not see the "big picture"
—focuses on something to the extent that all else is ignored
—inflexible

Reasons:

—parents are perfectionists or expect perfection
—taught to be detail-oriented
—does not recognize a middle ground; things are either black or white
—has attained perfection at something and feels there is no excuse for less
—may have an attention deficit
—may be compulsive
—looking for acceptance

Case Study:

Sholanda was given the task of doing the laundry at home. What would seem to be an easy, straightforward task for most people took her hours and hours to do. After sorting the clothes into different piles, she poured the exact amount of laundry detergent into the machine. She wasn't sure about the water temperatures, so she spent a half hour looking for the directions for the washing machine. After that was located, she started the first load. Halfway through, she realized that she might have tossed in a new pair of jeans that would probably color the other clothes. She took it out and restarted the load. When it came to drying the clothes, she didn't move from the laundry room because she wanted to be there for the exact moment the clothes came out of the dryer. After taking the clothes out, she ironed each and every piece—even her athletic socks and her underwear. When it came time to hang up her shirts, she put each one on a hanger and put it on the line drawn on the wooden rod of her closet—one line for each shirt.

Things to Try:

For the student

1. Get in touch with time. How long should each task take? How long does it take for you to complete?
2. What things are important to be done perfectly? What can be done *adequately* without spending too much time on it?
3. Look for gray areas or moderation in things. When is it OK to compromise?
4. Use your strengths—without overdoing it!

For the teacher

1. Give student an estimate of time involved in completing a project.
2. Be clear on standards for grading.
3. Give student a creative outlet (when your work is done, you can make a poster).
4. Show student how to correct minor mistakes without redoing the entire project.
5. Discuss when perfection is possible and desirable; when should this be our goal? (spelling tests, speech, math paper, etc.)
6. If you give open-ended assignments, help student focus on what the ending or final project will be or look like (make an endpoint).

For the parent

1. Demonstrate for your child how you want a specified task performed.
2. Set specific limits—"Don't spend more than 10 minutes on this."
3. Realize that some people find safety and security in organization and rituals; this is fine as long as it doesn't interfere with day-to-day living.
4. Praise your child for accomplishing tasks within his/her limits—"You're done with your math. Now you've got time to watch TV."

Activity #1: Case Study

Use Worksheet #41, "Battle Plan," with students to give ideas for how Sholanda can complete a task, do it well, and do it efficiently.

Activity #2: Personal Application

If students have a problem in this area, use Worksheet #41 to make a plan for changing behavior in this area.

Activity #3: Worksheet #52, A Perfect '10'

Synopsis: Some tasks are expected to be completed perfectly—and we expect to be praised for doing so. If a student is able to do something extremely well or has had a "golden moment" in which everything worked out perfectly, this can be a real self-esteem builder.

Directions: Students are to think of an experience or a talent they have in which they performed very well—maybe even perfectly. They are to draw a picture, write about it, or creatively express this experience.

Discussion Questions:

1. How did you feel when you felt you were perfect?
2. Did feeling perfect once make you want to be perfect again?
3. How did others react to your perfect performance or moment?

Journal-Entry Ideas

- If you could be perfect at something, what would it be? Why? Could it ever happen that you would achieve this?
- Who are some people who have been "perfect 10's" at something? What do you think it cost them (in time, effort, money) to reach this point?
- Here's a nightmare: You're sitting in front of the piano, ready to play a difficult piece you had memorized for the 10,000 people who are watching you on stage. You take a deep breath, lift your fingers . . . and your mind goes blank. Describe how you feel. What will you do?

Name____ Date ______________

A Perfect "10"

Worksheet #52

Directions: Draw, write, or convey in whatever means you want, something you have done that came pretty close to perfect—depending on what standard is necessary to evaluate. This may be a perfect ride over a jumping course, a perfect dive, a perfect paper, playing a song on a guitar without a single mistake, or WHATEVER! Maybe it only happened once . . . but it happened!

"It Was Perfect"

Lesson 32: "I can't control my emotions."

Examples of Behavior:

—easily provoked to temper tantrums

—cries easily

—overreacts to situations; "flies off the handle"

—may experience emotions without identifiable cause

—acts first, thinks later

—means what he/she says at the time, later regrets it or changes mind

—acts like Jekyll and Hyde

Reasons:

—doesn't think logically

—receives attention for acting out

—bad temper modeled by others

—emotionally immature

—may have truly traumatic situations to deal with

—short-sighted; does not see an end to events

Case Study:

Lucas was generally a nice, easy-going guy, but occasionally something would trigger his temper and he would change into a nasty, foul-mouthed creature. Other students hesitated before they approached him, because they weren't sure what mood he was going to be in. What would make him laugh one day would set him off into a screaming frenzy the next. You never knew what to expect! "Lucas, you've got to control your temper!" the principal warned him after he had been sent to the office for the second time in a day for fighting with another student and being disrespectful to the teacher. "You're going to hit somebody sometime and really get yourself in a lot of trouble." Lucas just shrugged. "My dad will take care of whoever tries to boss me around, and that includes you. This is just the way I am."

Things to Try:

For the student

1. Identify what situations/people/events bring out the worst in you.
2. Plan ahead when stressful situations are coming up. What will you do when things go wrong?
3. Slow yourself down; don't let your emotions run ahead of you.
4. Be aware of people or things that help you calm down.
5. Think through a situation logically. Is it worth getting upset about?
6. Take out your anger/frustrations in appropriate ways (go for a walk, lift weights, run around the block, chop wood, etc.).
7. Be aware of stressors in your life. You may be overwhelmed by all that you have to deal with.
8. Sort through problems with a counselor, parent, or friend.

For the teacher

1. Give the temperamental student some space; work out a mutual plan to handle explosive moments (have student leave the room, put head down, go to the counselor, etc.).
2. Be available to talk to student at some point during the day.
3. Be sympathetic if student is experiencing family problems.
4. Refer student to the school counselor if this is appropriate.
5. Stay in touch with parents if they are receptive.
6. Provide class discussion for general exploration of how to handle stressful situations.

For the parent

1. Be a good role model of how to handle your emotions.
2. Explain that mature people keep their emotions in check.
3. Have your child think through situations. What is the logical outcome?
4. If possible, provide a quiet private place for your child to retreat to (bedroom, basement, etc.).
5. Praise your child for taking control of his/her emotions.

Activity #1: Case Study

Have students use Worksheet #41, "Battle Plan," to work through possible solutions for Lucas to use in dealing with runaway emotions.

Activity #2: Personal Application

If students are experiencing problems with controlling emotions, have them work through Worksheet #41 to come up with ideas.

Activity #3: Worksheet #53, The Colors of My Feelings

Synopsis: Students may associate strong colors with strong emotions. Black may represent sadness or depression; blue may represent happiness; etc. Students are to focus on different emotions and how they are conveyed through color.

Directions: Students are to select colors to represent various emotions. They are to actually color the worksheet using markers, colored pencils, or crayons.

Discussion Questions:

1. Did most people in the class pick the same colors to represent various emotions?
2. Why do you think dark colors are associated with sadness or unhappy emotions? *(funereal colors, dark days, bad weather, etc.)*
3. Why do you think light colors are associated with happier emotions? *(blue sky = nice day, lightness might seem like there is no burden, etc.)*
4. Do you find you wear certain colors on certain days, depending on how you feel?
5. How are colors used to describe certain situations? For example, having the blues, red-letter day, in the black/in the red, etc.

Journal-Entry Idea

- What color did you choose to represent the following emotions? Why did you select the color you did? How does that color make you feel?

a. anger	c. sadness	e. weariness
b. happiness	d. excitement	f. surprised

Name____________________________________ Date ______________

The Colors of My Feelings

Worksheet #53

Directions: What color would you choose to represent each emotion? Fill in the boxes below according to what color appeals to you.

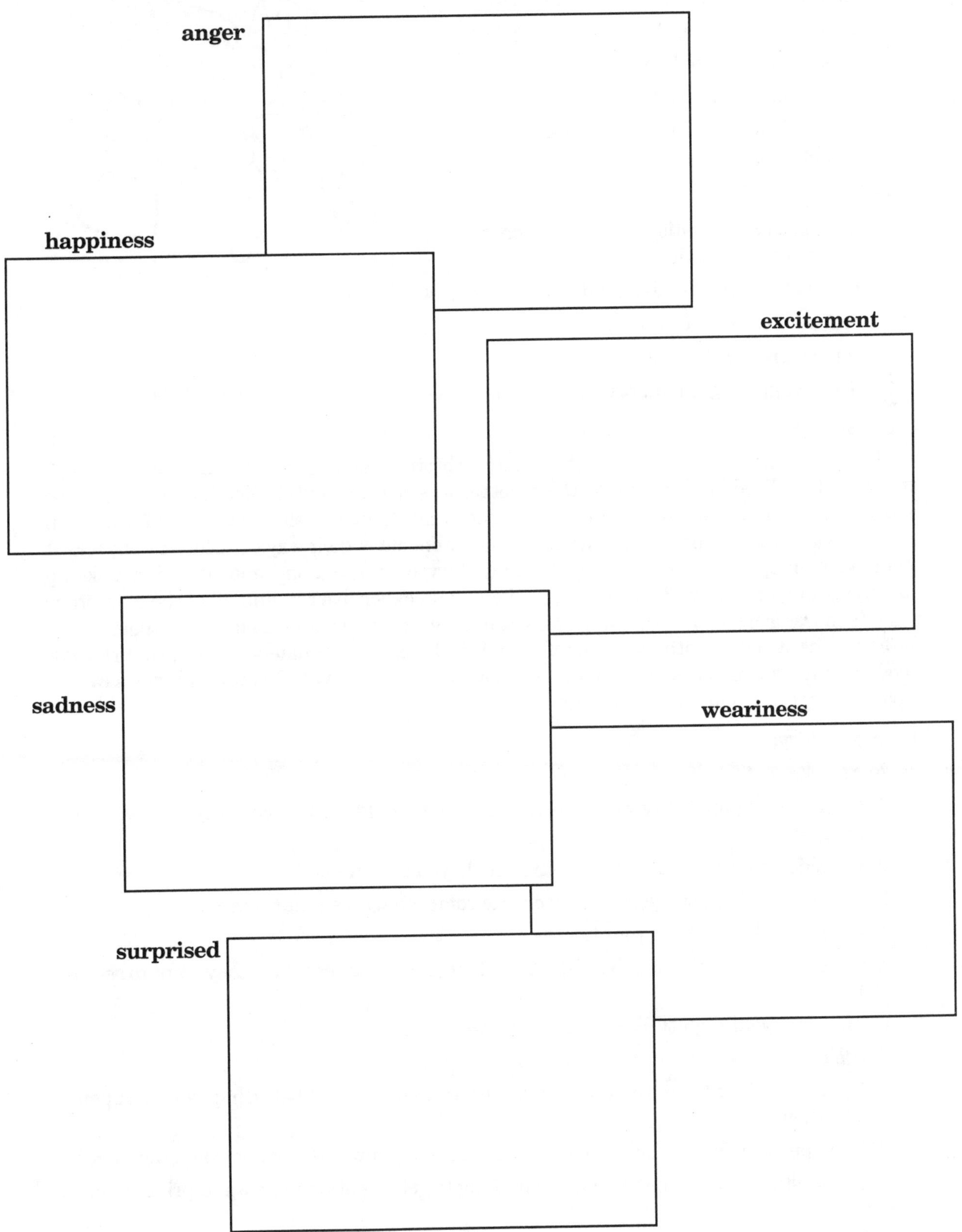

Lesson 33: "Other people don't like me."

Examples of Behavior:

—not picked for groups

—ignored by others

—makes negative comments about others

—may have abrasive, obnoxious personality

—tries too hard to be liked

—very quiet, not noticed by others

—takes advantage of other people's attention by rambling on and on

Reasons:

—not a good conversationalist; comes across as uninteresting and dull

—does not realize or understand how others react to him/her

—comes across as overbearing

—comes across as snobbish or aloof

—does not give a good impression

Case Study:

Brenda came from a poor family. She and her brothers and sisters were seen as "outcasts" at school. They lived in a little house, their mother was divorced and cleaned houses for a living, and their clothes were well-worn. Someone decided that Brenda smelled, and her fate was sewn up after that. Kids gave her unkind nicknames and went out of their way to make sure she wasn't included in group activities. Brenda was simply starved for attention—and started to make up stories about going out with guys at night, having an expensive car, and all of the glamorous things she was going to do on the weekends. It made everything worse, as now the students who didn't like her to begin with made fun of her fabrications. Unfortunately, students didn't know about Brenda's incredible artistic ability and how good she was with children. All they saw was a pathetic girl who told lies for attention.

Things to Try:

For the student

1. Consider: Is popularity worth the price? What would have to change about you to be accepted?
2. Consider: Do you want to be like the people you are around?
3. Focus on making one good friend; choose someone with similar interests.
4. Let people know about your talents.
5. Control your reaction to others; don't let them make you react how they want to see you. Be in control.
6. Maintain your dignity. Don't drop to a lower level.

For the teacher

1. Let the student know you are a protector; tormenting and belittling won't happen in YOUR class.
2. Don't push students to like each other, but prompt group participation whenever possible.
3. Praise student when he/she does something to get attention in an appropriate manner.

4. Help student "tone down" obnoxious behaviors; use role playing, social skills training, substitute more appropriate behaviors.
5. Incorporate the help (subtly) of a kind, mature student to help include student in activities.
6. Assign groups in random ways, such as numbering off, instead of having students pick who they want to be in a group.
7. Videotape students occasionally (performing a skit, reading a book report, etc.) so they can see how they actually look and come across to others.

For the parent

1. Encourage your child to have friends over and do things with others.
2. Realize that some children don't need to have a lot of friends; they prefer to be alone or with others of a different age.
3. Teach your child manners.
4. Encourage your child to maintain good manners and dignity despite what others may say about him/her.
5. Try to help your child fit in by helping or allowing him/her to look like the peer group (jeans, shoes, hair, etc.).
6. Make sure your child goes to school clean.

ACTIVITY #1: CASE STUDY

Use Worksheet #41, "Battle Plan," with students to work through possible solutions to help Brenda fit in with her peer group.

ACTIVITY #2: PERSONAL APPLICATION

Have students use Worksheet #41 to come up with various ideas for themselves if this is a personal problem.

ACTIVITY #3: WORKSHEET #54, CHOOSE ME!

Synopsis: Everyone has good and bad characteristics. Some students may not be chosen to be part of an "in" group simply because others do not know them well enough. It is important to learn more about a person before judging him or her.

Directions: Students are to select a fictitious partner for a project to be chosen from six characters on the worksheet. A brief personality sketch is provided for the characters. Students must select who they would most like to work with.

Discussion Questions:

1. Whom did you select and why?
2. Which personality characteristics of the characters did you find distasteful? Which were interesting?
3. What personality characteristics would be helpful for this sort of project?
4. If the project was something like putting on a comedy sketch for the school talent show, who might be a good partner?

Journal-Entry Ideas

- Write a creative advertisement for yourself, explaining why someone should take the time to get to know you. Tell about your interesting attributes!
- Who is someone whom you are pretty sure does not like you? How did this begin? Would you attribute this to a difference in personality, interests, a conflict at one time, a misunderstanding, or simply not knowing each other? Do you feel the same way about this person? Why?
- What is an act of kindness you could do specifically for someone who you think may not like you? What kind of reaction would you get from this person? Can you take a big risk and actually do it?

Name________________________________ Date ______________

Choose Me!

Worksheet #54

Directions: You have to choose a partner to work closely with on a social studies project. The project involves making a map, doing a field trip to locate places to put on the map, writing a report about your project, and presenting it to the class. Who would you pick to be your partner? Tell why or why not.

Dolores

She hates to write and would rather watch TV than do work, but she knows a lot of people and is very creative.

____

____

Ken

Ken is artistic and has his own darkroom for developing photos. He is very quiet and doesn't like to get up in front of people. You think he is pretty smart, but you don't know for sure.

____

____

Alfred

He tends to put things off until the last minute; but under pressure he really comes through and manages to get everything done. He's fun to be with, but you never know when he's going to give up and desert you.

____

____

Aimee

Aimee is an excellent student; she always gets A's on her reports and papers. She knows she is really smart and will tell you over and over how you should be doing your project.

____

____

David

David is a lot of fun. You will always find yourself laughing and having a good time with him. He likes to read, but only comic books and sports magazines.

____

____

Cara

Cara is an average student, but she misses a lot of school because of her allergies. She works well independently, and could probably do anything well if she was taught how to do it. She's willing to try . . . as long as she's not sneezing, sleeping, or at the medical clinic.

____

____

Lesson 34: "I hold grudges."

Examples of Behavior:

—insists he/she is right

—refuses to look at situation from another point of view

—hangs on to anger from a much earlier time or episode

—can't let something drop; must have last word

—intends to make "enemy" pay

—may not even have a clear recollection of the episode

Why were you so rude to that teacher?
I hate that teacher—she gave me an F in spelling when I was in third grade.
You had Mrs. Smith in third grade—that was Mrs. Jones!
Well—she's probably giving some poor kid an F anyway. She looks like Mrs. Smith!

Reasons:

—parents, family members, peers may "fuel the fire" to keep a grudge going

—taught that retaliation is fair and necessary

—unable to go beyond the point of argument; can't leap that hurdle emotionally

—enjoys the feeling of anger and continuing the animosity

Case Study:

Evelyn, a quiet and shy student, was giving an oral report in front of the members of her speech class, a required project for all students. While she was speaking, Carolyn, a pretty, popular student, was mimicking her movements and getting other students to laugh at her. Evelyn was not only embarrassed, she was shook up enough to forget her speech. The memory of how she felt stayed with her for weeks and built up the more she thought about it. Carolyn, meanwhile, hadn't even given the episode a second thought—it was completely forgotten. She didn't even particularly dislike Evelyn; she was just having a good time. As time went on, Evelyn became more vocal about how rude and stuck-up Carolyn (and all of her friends) were. Evelyn and her friends made lists of ways they were going to set Carolyn up to embarrass her. Every opportunity that came up found Evelyn bad-mouthing Carolyn. Later in the semester, Evelyn found that she and Carolyn were on the same side for a debate. Evelyn was so upset she asked the teacher if she could transfer to another class. The teacher was aware of the growing hostility and referred Evelyn to the school counselor, as this problem was not getting any better.

Things to Try:

For the student

1. Decide how important this grudge is to you. Is it worth the time, effort, and worry?
2. Realize that situations are reversible; you don't have to go through this agony forever.
3. Seek an impartial opinion. Could you be partly wrong?
4. Take steps for deciding how to resolve this problem.
5. Resolve to be honest and look at the situation with an open mind.
6. Are you willing to change your mind with more facts?
7. Are you overreacting?

For the teacher

1. Hold class discussions about how to resolve conflicts.
2. "Letting go" is a difficult, but necessary social skill; explain and demonstrate this to students.

3. Use the story of the Hatfields and the McCoys to illustrate pointlessness of long grudge-holding.
4. Emphasize the shortness of life, value of getting along and eliminating hateful feelings.
5. Provide exercises in seeing another point of view; show how perspective changes.

For the parent

1. If your child is unrealistic about a situation, seek help for him/her; don't let it grow.
2. If behavior seems potentially destructive and harmful, intervene immediately.
3. Don't buy into plans for retaliation; be an adult! Don't encourage or help your child plan to "get back" at someone.
4. Be available to listen to your child; he/she may feel better by talking about it.
5. Be sympathetic, but offer suggestions for getting past this grudge; don't live in the past.
6. Ask your child: "Will this be important ten years from now?"

Activity #1: Case Study

Have students use Worksheet #41, "Battle Plan," to come up with a potential plan for Evelyn to use to get over her grudge against Carolyn.

Activity #2: Personal Application

Have students work through ideas on Worksheet #41 if this is a problem area for them.

Activity #3: Worksheet #55, Drawing the Line

Synopsis: Grudges can fester and grow for years, leading to wasted time, unhappiness, and broken relationships. It takes strength to be the one to start making amends. Over time, grudges can grow to be something unhealthy and pointless.

Directions: Students are to read the story about two individuals who hold a grudge against each other which lasts for years. Students are given a timeline of events that occurred after the incident began. They are to draw a line where they think the individuals should have let go of the grudge and started talking to each other.

Discussion Questions:

1. Why don't people just forget about grudges over time? Why do some people hang on to them?
2. Do you think most grudges begin over something small and insignificant? Does time make a difference?
3. If your feelings are hurt and you can identify specifically the person who hurt your feelings or made you feel embarrassed, upset, or stupid, what are other ways you could handle the situation?
4. Do you think men and women handle anger against other people in different ways? Are men more open? More prone to fight about it? Are women more likely to hold grudges? More prone to quietly plot about how to get back at someone?

Journal-Entry Ideas

- Who do you hold (or have you held) a grudge against? What started the problem? Did you ever resolve it? Now that you look back, does it seem important?
- What are some ways you show your dislike or anger against someone? Are you open about it or more subtle?
- Do you think there is anyone who is holding a grudge against you right now? Who might it be and what could the problem be? Do you intend to do anything differently to resolve the situation?

Name_______________________________________ Date ______________

Drawing the Line

Worksheet #55

Directions: Read about a Grudge Match below. Draw a line where you think the two individuals should give up their grudges.

Tomas and Lee had been friends for a long time. They both played on the school basketball team and often spent time together shooting pool, riding their bikes, and working on restoring an old motorcycle that belonged to Lee's older brother. One day Tomas was sick from school with a cold and didn't hear the announcement that basketball practice was required the next day or players would be cut. Lee had had a hard day at school that day—he struggled with a test, was missing two assignments, and didn't feel well himself. In all of the chaos, he forgot to tell Tomas about the basketball announcement. Tomas stayed home from school the next day and found that he was cut from the basketball team.

7:00 P.M.: Tomas called Lee on the phone. Tomas blamed Lee for not telling him about the announcement. Lee insisted that he had simply forgotten, and that Tomas should have remembered anyway because the coach had made that announcement about cuts at the beginning of the season. Tomas was angry and said that Lee was a rotten friend. Lee hung up.

8 A.M. the next morning: Lee and Tomas did not speak to each other at school. The morning announcements named the players who made the team. Lee was one of them. Tomas, of course, was not.

10:30 A.M.: Players came up to Tomas, wondering why he didn't make the team. Tomas blamed Lee in front of them, stating that he didn't tell him about the announcement. The players were sympathetic, insisting that Tomas would have made the team.

3:30 P.M.: During practice, Lee missed a few easy shots. Some of the other players made comments that Tomas should have made the team instead of Lee.

Two days later: Lee and Tomas continued to avoid each other. Tomas began showing up to watch practice. When Lee missed a shot, Tomas laughed loudly. Lee swore at him. The coach told Tomas to leave and not return to watch any practices.

The first game: Lee made several important plays during the game. The players who had been sympathetic with Tomas now had forgotten about him and were slapping Lee on the back, giving him a nickname, and inviting him to shoot baskets over the weekend.

A month later: Lee and Tomas had no contact with each other at all. Whenever Lee did something good in a game, Tomas bad-mouthed him and even "boo-ed" at the games. He was asked to leave by the school principal.

Months later: Tomas began hanging around with rougher kids who didn't attend sports at all; in fact, they rarely attended school. While Lee continued to perform well in basketball and tried out for other sports, Tomas began to get a reputation as someone who hung out with gang members.

Summer: Lee's home was vandalized one weekend when the family was visiting relatives—the motorcycle was stolen, drawers were ransacked, money was missing, and Lee's room was ripped apart. Lee's family called the police and told them to check out Tomas and his buddies. Through other people, Tomas's story was that he had nothing to do with that incident.

A year later: Tomas had dropped out of school and was working at a factory. During a freak accident, there was an explosion of a furnace and he was burned over his chest and arms. The entire community took up a collection and had a fundraiser to try to make money to pay for his medication expenses. Lee did not contribute to raising any money for that "criminal."

Five years later: Lee graduated from college and was home for the summer, working at his father's office. One of his duties was to screen applicants for part-time positions. It turned out that Tomas was one of the applicants. Lee didn't even bother to look at the application. He tossed it into the wastebasket.

Ten years later: Lee and Tomas both had daughters in the same kindergarten class at the local elementary school. When they passed each other in the hallway during conference time, they walked past each other as though they were invisible.

Ten years after that: Lee's business has gone bankrupt and his wife left him (with their daughter). He is living in a small apartment, drinking too much, trying to figure out what to do with his life. Meanwhile, Tomas went to night school, got his G.E.D., and now owns a hardware store that is doing quite well. When Tomas ran into Lee in the parking lot one day,

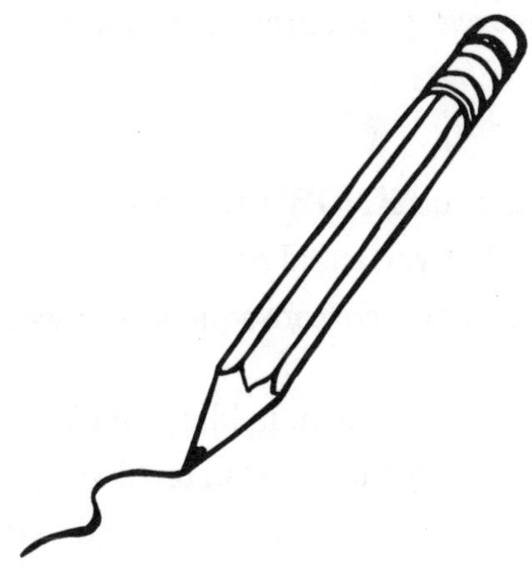

Lesson 35: "I do things that will get me in trouble."

Examples of Behavior:

—hangs around with friends who are in trouble

—gets into trouble at school with teachers, other students

—impulsive; doesn't think first

—makes the same mistakes over and over

—very susceptible to peer pressure

—craves excitement

Reasons:

—does not understand or envision consequences of actions

—low tolerance for waiting; needs immediate gratification

—very close connections with peers who are often in trouble

—views encounters with authority figures as a challenge

—does not respect authority figures

—little restraint or limits at home

—immature

Case Study:

Isaac was a very intelligent boy, but a poor student who was always getting into trouble. He was a part of a group that had a reputation as being rough and tough. When someone from the group had an idea for having fun (usually one that involved breaking a rule of the school or society), he was the first one to get involved. One day several of the boys were in the restroom. They figured out a way to pull down some of the ceiling tiles and were exploring the pipes and wiring in the ceiling. They thought maybe they could figure out a way to turn on the automatic sprinklers. When they were caught, everyone credited Isaac with the idea. "Why can't you say 'no' to your friends?" asked the assistant principal. "Do you really enjoy getting into trouble all the time? Why can't you use your intelligence to do something more constructive?" Isaac shrugged his shoulders. "With a little more time, I probably could have figured it out," he said. "That would have been really cool—to have everyone sprayed with water."

Things to Try:

For the student

1. Make a list of the things you KNOW will get you into trouble.
2. Decide ahead of time what you could do to avoid getting involved in that situation.
3. Think through possible (probable) consequences of what you are interested in doing, but hesitant.
4. Are your friends bringing you down, holding you back?
5. Change your situation! Don't get involved in problems that are likely to get you into trouble.
6. Make a list of ten things you could do for fun and excitement that won't hurt anybody or yourself.

For the teacher

1. Don't lecture; question student on his/her thinking and try to arrive at a logical theory. ("If I do this, this will probably happen.")

2. If student is in potentially dangerous situations, explain why it is harmful and dangerous.
3. Invite a police officer to talk to the class about the necessity of having rules and following them.
4. Try to intervene if you see student is headed for trouble (talk, explain, listen, etc.).
5. There is probably a teacher or administrator on staff who had a wild childhood—invite him/her to tell some anecdotes and give a moral to the story.

For the parent

1. Give clear, consistent limits for what is acceptable in your household.
2. Explain fair and likely consequences for breaking rules.
3. Involve your child in forming rules and consequences as much as is appropriate.
4. Explain how your child getting into trouble also affects and hurts other members of the family.
5. Help your child make changes in the situation (friends, settings, events) as much as possible.

Activity #1: Case Study

Students can use Worksheet #41, "Battle Plan," to make suggestions for Isaac to stop getting into preventative trouble.

Activity #2: Personal Application

Have students use Worksheet #41 to make a plan for helping themselves stay clear of trouble.

Activity #3: Worksheet #56, Trouble Magnets

Synopsis: Certain things will draw or attract trouble for certain individuals. Students should be aware of this. Awareness in conjunction with desire to change can help the student avoid these kinds of problems.

Directions: Students are to identify what things/people/situations have a tendency to get them into trouble. They are to draw or write a brief description of this item. (*Caution:* In order to avoid name calling, blaming others, or truly incriminating themselves, you may want to assure students that this will be treated as confidential.)

Discussion Questions:

1. Why do people continue to do things they know will get them into trouble, especially if they have gotten into trouble in the past?
2. How much can you really blame another person for "making you get in trouble"? Aren't people ultimately accountable for their own actions?
3. Why is it hard to change friends if you know that the group you hang around with will lead to trouble?

Journal-Entry Ideas

- What is the most amount of trouble you have gotten into? Was it at school, home, in the community? Were you caught? What was your punishment? Would you do it again?
- What would be the best way for you to break your trouble magnet? What would have to happen to you in order for you to stop getting into this kind of trouble?
- In some ways, do you want to do something bad and then get caught? Do you think some people feel this way? Why?

Trouble Magnets

Worksheet #56

Directions: What things attract you that you know will have a tendency to get you into trouble? Draw a picture or write a brief comment that describes each.

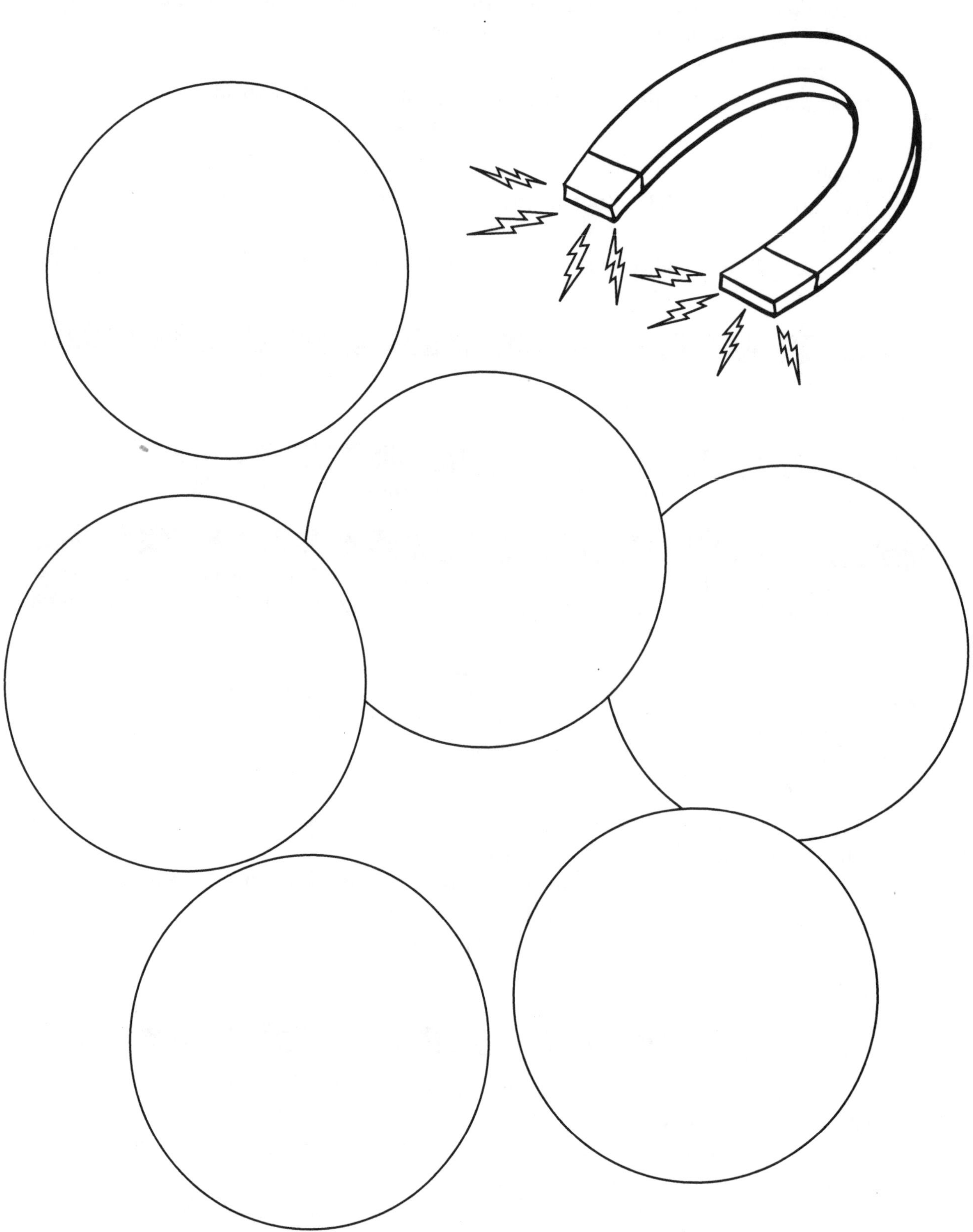

Lesson 36: "I'm afraid to take a risk."

Examples of Behavior:

—looks for the easy way out

—never does extra credit work

—only does what he/she is sure of

—hesitant to give answers, opinions

—not confident with answers given

What are you working so hard on, Thelma?
I'm figuring out how many problems I can get wrong and still get a D- to pass!

Reasons:

—afraid of failure

—may have been embarrassed or ridiculed over a failed risk

—lazy; low energy level

—not motivated by grades or external reinforcers

—unstable; frightening home life or problems

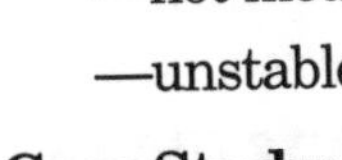

Case Study:

Mai was an average student in social studies. She usually got at least a "C" on her tests, reports, and daily work. Although her teacher offered the entire class the opportunity to improve their grades by doing extra credit maps, reports, and other projects, Mai was satisfied with her mediocre grade and spent any extra class time reading a novel or writing notes to her friends. In the spring, she decided to try out for the tennis team. She was informed that she had to have a "B" average to even try out for the team. Suddenly, it was important to get a "B" or better in every class. The social studies teacher told students that during the next grading period, they would have the opportunity to get quite a few extra points for bringing in news articles and writing short summaries about them. Mai decided she would rather watch TV at night than go through the newspaper, cutting out articles. (Her father always complained about the holes, anyway.) "Don't you want to go out for tennis?" asked her sister. "I thought you were going to try to make the team?" Mai shook her head and turned on the remote control. "I probably wouldn't make the team anyway," she said.

Things to Try:

For the student

1. Take a small risk first; build up your confidence that you can do it.
2. Push yourself; go a little farther than you originally intended.
3. Focus 100% on one goal. Make a commitment to achieve!
4. Enlist the help of a friend or partner to help you stick with it.
5. Initiate asking the help of another person who can do what you want to do.
6. Keep a written record of your successes, no matter how small.
7. Be reasonable—don't risk everything for a foolish gamble.

For the teacher

1. Provide opportunities for students to take risks.
2. Study famous risk-takers; consider the outcomes and cost.
3. Inform/remind students that everyone learns from mistakes; in fact, sometimes making a mistake is a good way to learn (give examples).
4. Set up tasks so that it is easier for students to succeed than to fail (make the failure option unpleasant).

5. Don't forget about the powerful impact of motivation.
6. Give some latitude when assigning extra credit ("Pick one of the three following projects," etc.).
7. Build up students' confidence ("Remember how well you did last time?").
8. Discuss positive (win-win) risks vs. foolish risks.
9. Offer opportunities for "playful risks"—art projects, skits, etc.

For the parent

1. Ask your child about extra credit options; check with teacher.
2. Share your personal fears about risk-taking with your child; model how you handle the situation.
3. Try to "quantify" risks—small, low-cost risk vs. huge, irreversible risk.
4. Support your child's efforts for taking positive risks.
5. Insist that if your child decides to take a risk, he/she sticks with it for a reasonable length of time before giving up (e.g., piano lessons, participating in a play, going to new youth group, etc.).

Activity #1: Case Study

Use Worksheet #41, "Battle Plan," to help guide students through making a plan for Mai to take some academic risks to improve her grades and a personal risk to try out for the tennis team.

Activity #2: Personal Application

Have students work through ideas using Worksheet #41 if this is a personal concern for them.

Activity #3: Worksheet #57, What's Behind Door #2?

Synopsis: Some risks are simply not worth the effort; others may yield vast rewards. It is a good idea to consider all sides of a risk—weigh the cost and outcome. Find out as much as you can!

Directions: Students are to select one of six doors that are on the worksheet and represent something that can be gained. The cost of each door is given.

Answers:

Door #1 — a bottle of vitamins. *Door #2* — a large, colored postcard of a Florida vacation. *Door #3* — a puppy from the local animal shelter (all fees have been waived). *Door #4* — an old pearl necklace that belonged to your great-grandmother and was given to her as a wedding gift from her great-grandmother; it has survived travel through several countries, wars, and a fire; it is given to you after the death of your mother. *Door #5* — a college diploma from a major university. *Door #6* — a lottery ticket worth $16 million.

Discussion Questions:

1. What factors did you consider before choosing your door?
2. Were you disappointed when you found out what was behind your door? Was it worth the cost?
3. Did you feel you were misled by any of the clues about the doors?
4. What were you thinking might be behind each door?

Journal-Entry Ideas

- What is the biggest risk you have taken? How did it turn out?
- Would you risk these things for something you really wanted?

  —your health

  —your safety

  —someone else's safety

  —money you have now

  —money you expect to get in the future

  —being in pain

  —being embarrassed in front of people you know

  —being embarrassed in front of people you don't know

  —getting yelled at

  —being late for something
- Make a list of some small, medium, and big risks. **Examples:**

  small — eating a cupcake made by your sister; wearing clothes that are not quite popular yet

  medium — getting on a horse that several people have said is "spirited"; crossing a busy highway

  big — walking across an ice-covered lake with a few holes in it; taking unknown drugs given to you by someone you don't know

Name________________________________ Date ____________

What's Behind Door #2?

Worksheet #57

Directions: How much are you willing to risk for the possible benefits that that risk will give you? Read the descriptions of what's behind each door and what's required to open the door. Decide which door (if any) you want.

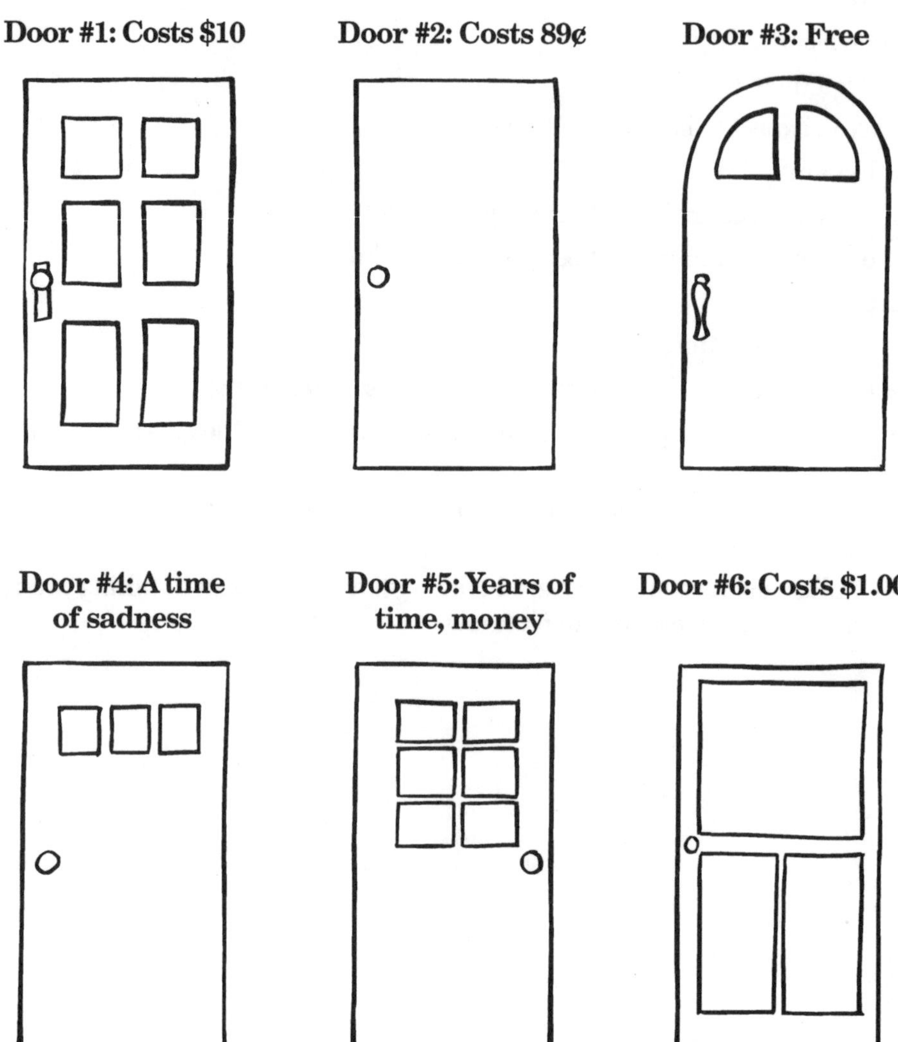

Door #1: Behind this door is something that will ensure your good health. You'll feel great!

Door #2: This contains something associated with relaxing, having a wonderful time, good meals, and feeling completely at ease.

Door #3: If you want to be loved and experience true friendship, you'll want this door.

Door #4: This is an item of incredible value. It holds the treasure of a lifetime.

Door #5: If you pay a little now, this will increase in value over time. Wait, and it will be worth a lot.

Door #6: This is a small piece of paper. It has the power to change your life.

Lesson 37: "I don't deserve anything better than this."

Examples of Behavior:

—satisfied with low grades

—not upset with poor quality of projects

—rushes through assignments and projects

—accepts status quo; does not initiate change

—has low standards for achievement

—does not expect much from others

Reasons:

—has been told he/she is not worth the time, effort, trouble

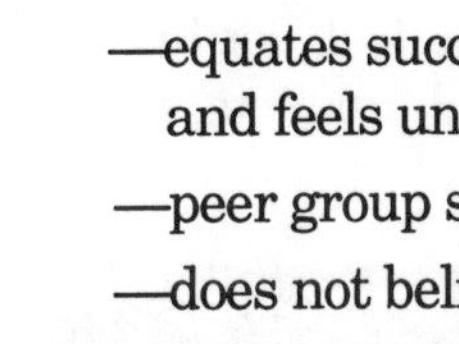

—equates success with achievement, and feels unsuccessful

—peer group shares same low expectations

—does not believe anything better is attainable

—cannot critically evaluate a situation; does not see the worth of something

Case Study:

Cynthia came from a poor family. Her father had left the home years earlier, and much of Cynthia's free time was spent babysitting her five younger brothers and sisters. Success in school was not a priority for anyone in her family or among her friends. She was quite vocal about her interest in going out with a lot of guys, especially older men. "Hey, at least somebody is interested in me," she told her teacher who was concerned that she was getting overly involved with an older man who was married and had a pregnant wife. "I must be attractive if I can get a guy who is already married to notice me. It's not that I don't care about his wife or anything, but she doesn't pay enough attention to him. It's her own fault."

Things to Try:

For the student

1. Be aware of the potential and real dangers of your situation.
2. Decide to WAIT for something that is worth waiting for.
3. Think through the rewards of delaying gratification of something that seems good now.
4. Set your sights higher than you think is possible; focus on something harder than you think you can achieve.
5. Start reading positive books, stories, and anecdotes. Fill your mind with healthy, inspirational thoughts.
6. Decide to believe in yourself, trust yourself.

For the teacher

1. Reaffirm the worth of each individual student in whatever method is appropriate for him/her and comfortable for you.
2. Talk individually to students who are in trouble or are dabbling with danger; refer to counselors if possible.
3. Don't hesitate to report suspected abuse or neglect to proper authorities.

4. Some students may need a "kick start" to wake up. Clearly, firmly inform them that they deserve better.
5. Talk about the meaning of "pride," what it means to have self-respect.
6. Inform students that life is not always fair; what is meted out to us may simply seem arbitrary or have nothing to do with what we deserved; however, sometimes we get *better* than we deserve.
7. Teach that life itself is a gift—discover your purpose.
8. Read and study stories of people who overcame the odds to become successful.

For the parent

1. Don't be overly critical of your child; this may backfire ("You should hang out with a better class of friends.")
2. Point out possible avenues of success (get out of this neighborhood/town by getting a good job/education).
3. Constantly reaffirm your child's worth to yourself, your family, and to society; show that you believe in him/her.
4. Sometimes it is good (and necessary) to shop around until you get the best deal; don't accept less (e.g., a better boyfriend, a better grade, better quality of clothes and products, etc.).
5. Teach your child to expect better of yourself and others.

Activity #1: Case Study

Have students examine Worksheet #41, "Battle Plan," to go through possible ideas for Cynthia to improve her situation.

Activity #2: Personal Application

Have students work through Worksheet #41 if this is an area of concern to them personally.

Activity #3: Worksheet #58, Getting What I Deserve

Synopsis: Sometimes we don't get what we deserve—luckily! In many cases, however, something such as a grade, points, or money is given as a direct relationship to the quality of the product or service (e.g., a test, a game, a tip). It can be a helpful exercise in judgment and clarifying values to come up with a rating scale and then measure some examples against that scale.

Directions: Students are given a brief description of the assignments that six fictitious characters have turned in. They are to assign a grade (letter or numerical) to each.

Discussion Questions:

1. What rating system did you use to grade the assignments?
2. Which assignments did you think were the best? Why?
3. To which assignments would you give a lower grade? Why?
4. What factors would you have to specify to your students in order to make it clear what your rating scale consists of?

Journal-Entry Ideas

- What are some things you don't have that you feel you deserve? Why do you deserve them?
- Have you ever gotten an award, money, or something else because someone felt you deserved it? What?
- Pretend you are giving an acceptance speech for being the "Student of the Year." Do you deserve the award? Let's hear the speech . . .

Name______________________________ Date ______________

Getting What I Deserve

Worksheet #58

Directions: Each of these students was given the same assignment. Look over what each turned in and put them in the order you think shows *best* to *worst*. Assign a grade to each.

Assignment: Interview someone you don't know very well. Find out what that person is interested in, a little bit about his/her past, and what he/she is doing now.

☐

Carlo's Work: He interviewed the mayor of the city. He followed the mayor around for a day, took photographs of the mayor talking to people, and tape recorded the interview. He typed up his interview and made several copies for anyone who was interested.

☐

Amanda's Work: She forgot to do the assignment, but she was going to interview a professional basketball player.

☐

David's Work: David interviewed his older brother. They share a room at home. He gave the brother a list of five questions and had him write down his answers on the sheet of paper which he handed in.

☐

Kaneesha's Work: She interviewed a new teacher at the school. She visited the teacher at her home and asked 20 questions, mostly about what the teacher's interests were. She found out that the teacher was active in raising golden retriever puppies that are later used for training to help blind people. She typed up her interview.

☐

Allen's Work: Allen interviewed a local doctor who performs a new kind of eye surgery that helps people see without glasses. After collecting brochures and watching a videotape, Allen talked to some patients who had had the surgery to find out about their reaction to the surgery. Then he went to the library to make some drawings of the eye. He also included some drawings of the parts of the ear, the tongue, and the nose.

☐

Debra's Work: Debra took a videocamera and interviewed a homeless person in a park. She found out that he used to be part of a wealthy family in another state. She showed the videotape to the class as her report.

Lesson 38: "I can't make decisions."

Examples of Behavior:

—puts off making decisions; procrastinates

—spends exorbitant amount of time considering alternatives

—changes mind constantly

—has no basis or plan for coming to a conclusion

—follows others' behavior, decisions

—begins a course of action, then gives up

—places too much importance on minor decisions

Reasons:

—does not trust own judgment

—rarely given opportunity to exercise choice or power

—has failed when making decisions; lacks confidence

—does not seek out information to support decision

—easily influenced by opinions of others

—easily influenced by pieces of information

—dependent on parent's opinions, influence

Case Study:

Alex had to ask his mother each morning what he should wear. Both realized that he would probably miss the bus if someone didn't take charge of making that first decision, as Alex would lose himself in time staring at the closet, unable to decide what to wear. At school, Alex did much better if the teachers gave him a specific, outlined assignment with clear directions, expectations, and deadlines. If he was given a choice of three different projects (and expected to be creative!), he was lost. Instead of beginning a project, he would start one of them (after agonizing over which one to pick) and then give up soon after he started. "Why don't they just tell me what to do?" Alex complained. "How am I supposed to know what to do?"

Things to Try:

For the student

1. Decide how much time should be devoted to making the decision. Is it long-lasting? Reversible? Will it affect me for a long time?
2. Does the decision need to be made right now? How much time do you have?
3. Do you need to gather more information to make a better decision?
4. Make a decision, then stick with it. Allow yourself a reasonable length of time to see the outcome or which way it's going before you change your mind or plan.
5. Talk it over with a friend, parent, or other adult.

For the teacher

1. Encourage student to make decisions; praise him/her for making attempts.
2. Provide opportunities for students to develop and use divergent, creative thinking. Expose students to open-ended problems.
3. Teach decision-making skills by using cooperative activities.
4. Give examples of looking at a problem from different points of view.

5. Present a position, then have student give the "other side"; how could someone see this differently?

For the parent

1. Allow your child to make decisions. Start small (what are you going to wear today/do after school/write your report on?) and encourage more important decisions (what will you spend this money on/which job are you going to take after school/how will you be able to play football and do the school play?).
2. As opportunities come up, have your child state an alternative point of view (use local news, TV reports, national events involving other countries, etc.).
3. Don't give your opinion and expect your child to fall in line. Encourage your child to think through all sides and come to a decision.
4. Realize that you may have to stand back, be quiet, and watch your child's poor decision fall through.
5. Talk about which decisions are reversible and which are not.
6. Put a time limit on some decisions that need to be resolved.

Activity #1: Case Study

Use Worksheet #41, "Battle Plan," to have students work through possible ideas for Alex to try to quit procrastinating and make some decisions.

Activity #2: Personal Application

Have students use Worksheet #41 to come up with a plan for making decisions if this is a concern for them.

Activity #3: Worksheet #59, Making Decisions

Synopsis: Decision-making can be facilitated by considering the importance and relative significance of the decision and all that it involves. Whereas some decisions may be of a minor nature, short-lived, and have little impact on many people, others will affect many people for a long time.

Directions: Students are given several situations in which a decision must be made. They are to decide how important the decision is to the individual, what information may be necessary to make a better decision, and whether or not the student (personally) is qualified to make that decision.

Discussion Questions:

1. What are some examples of small, relatively unimportant decisions that people make everyday?
2. Can you think of some recent decisions that have been made politically that affect the world? How about national decisions?
3. What are some jobs or careers that depend heavily upon making decisions for other people?
4. Why do you think it is hard to make some unpopular decisions even though that decision may be the "right" one?

Journal-Entry Ideas

- What are the last ten decisions you have had to make? Score each according to how "important" that decision was. How did your decisions turn out?
- What would you do if you felt very strongly about a certain point of view, but you knew it would be very unpopular; would you tell others how you felt or keep quiet? What if you were the one who had to make the unpopular decision? What would you do?

Name____ Date ______________

Making Decisions

Worksheet #5

Directions: Decide (a) how important the following decisions are; (b) what further information would be necessary or helpful to make a good decision; and (c) whether or not YOU are qualified to make that decision.

1. An elderly man seated at the table next to you is choking—there might be something caught in his throat. Should you perform the Heimlich maneuver?

(a) ____

(b) ____

(c) ____

2. It's Saturday and you and your friends are going outside to play football in the mud. Should you wear your favorite old jeans or your sweats?

(a) ____

(b) ____

(c) ____

3. It's your parents' 25th wedding anniversary and you are in charge of throwing them a surprise party. What's it going to be like?

(a) ____

(b) ____

(c) ____

4. You finally got your high school diploma. Yeaaaa! Dad tells you that you must either get a job or go to college or other advanced training. What's it going to be?

(a) ____

(b) ____

(c) ____

Lesson 39: "I'm wonderful; you're not so great."

Examples of Behavior:

—constantly bragging about self and accomplishments

—putting others down, pointing out their weaknesses

—exaggerates and embellishes stories about self

—demands attention

—very critical of others and their actions

—looks down on others; appears snobbish

—finds fault with others

Reasons:

—not objective about situations; perspective is very one-sided

—told by parents and family that he/she is better than others

—feels better when others are put down

—does not receive genuine compliments or praise from others

—tries to cover up feelings of low self-worth; masks true feelings

Case Study:

Sophia's parents, though divorced, were each independently wealthy. Her mother owned a profitable cleaning service and her father was a business administrator in a large company. Both were highly educated, successful, and demanding. Though they never said so, Sophia sometimes felt that her parents were disappointed in her since she did not do well in school. She was relieved when the parents chose to blame the school system and the teachers for her failure to be more successful in school. Sophia did not have a lot of friends, possibly because she labeled fellow students as "stupid" and "boring." Each day Sophia came to school dressed in expensive clothes and jewelry. "School is a drag," she laughed to her classmates. "My parents did just fine and neither one of them went to college. I don't have time to study—not while there's shopping to be done!"

Things to Try:

For the student

1. Realize how many times a day you blame others/brag about yourself/put others down. Be aware of what you are saying and doing.
2. Ask a friend or peer to help you evaluate your behavior. How does what you say or do come across to others? Is this your intent?
3. Before you start blaming someone, think of at least two possible explanations.
4. Realize that sometimes you will be blamed unfairly; don't let it throw you!
5. Become an encourager to others instead of a blamer—see what happens!

For the teacher

1. Discuss what a "tattle-tale" is and why this is unpopular and unhelpful.
2. When a student starts to brag obnoxiously about him-/herself, help the student "tone it down" to be more realistic.
3. Give each student a one-minute opportunity occasionally to tell something about him-/herself (e.g., "Tell me something you did that was interesting this weekend.").

4. Realize that although the student tries to come across as proud and arrogant, he/she is really quite the opposite—understand this need.
5. Do not allow "put downs" in your classroom.

For the parent

1. Be objective about your child's skills and abilities. Don't complain that he/she should have been first, should have won, etc.
2. Support the teacher and school in their attempts to instruct your child. If you have complaints, handle them with the people involved rather than "tear down" these adults in front of your child.
3. Don't be an obnoxious parent, constantly bragging about your child (others may not feel the same way about your "perfect" child).
4. Don't chime in too quickly when your child finds fault with someone else. Ask him/her if she got the facts, why he/she feels this way, etc. Do some investigating.
5. Realize that bragging is a symptom of a low self-esteem. Try to find positive, sincere ways to praise your child.

Activity #1: Case Study

Use Worksheet #41, "Battle Plan," to have students come up with some ideas for Sophia to try to quit being so critical of others and more positive about herself.

Activity #2: Personal Application

Have students work through ideas using Worksheet #41 to come up with ideas to try if this is a problem for them.

Activity #3: Worksheet #60, I'm GRRRRRRREAT!!

Synopsis: It is fine to convey our strengths and good points to others, but sometimes the manner and words chosen can portray a completely different demeanor—it may come across as bragging and conceit. The manner in which we say things is important in setting the tone for what others hear and react to.

Directions: Several characters and their comments are portrayed on the worksheet. Students are to circle the ones who are telling good things about themselves in a nice way; they are to put an X on the characters who appear to be bragging or are obnoxious to others.

Answers: 1. X; 2. 0; 3. 0; 4. X; 5. 0; 6. X.

Discussion Questions:

1. How can someone tell about his/her exciting accomplishments without coming across as bragging or conceited?
2. Why do you think some people put others down in an attempt to build themselves up? Does it really make them feel better?
3. Can you think of someone who credited someone else with his/her success? A parent, coach, best friend?
4. When was the last time you heard someone say, "It's not my fault!" What were the circumstances? Who got blamed? Was this fair?
5. When was the last time you heard someone say, "It was my fault. I'll take responsibility for that." What were the circumstances? How did you feel about this person?

Journal-Entry Ideas

- What is something you know you are really good at? How could you let other people know about this without coming across as being obnoxious?
- Do you tend to be overly critical of a certain person or group of people? Why do you feel this way? What specifically do you find yourself doing around this person or group of people? What satisfaction do you feel from your behavior?
- When has someone been critical of you or really put you down? How did you react?

Name________________________________ Date ____________

I'm GRRRRRRRREAT!!

Worksheet #6

Directions: Circle the characters below who are telling good things about themselves in a nice way. Put an X on the ones who are being braggarts.

1.

I scored three touchdowns at the last game. No one could come close to me! I'm sure I'll get the most valuable player award—if I don't, the coach is blind.
22

2.

This is my science project. It's a little volcano that really erupts. I was awarded a blue ribbon for one of the best exhibits in the school.

3.

I have a lot of friends. I don't know if I'll have room for everyone in my basement when I have my birthday party. I like everybody and seem to get along with guys and girls. I think there is something nice about everyone, and everyone is my friend.

4.

There are some girls in this place who just don't know how to dress. I took modeling classes and I read fashion magazines so I know what is "in." I know I look fabulous.

5.

I'm really good at playing the saxophone. I've taken lessons for years and years, so I guess I should be. I love to perform and I'll play for you right now if you've got a minute! Hold on! You'll enjoy this!

6.

My dog is a very rare breed imported from Europe. He was extremely expensive. I don't let just anyone take care of him. He's much too valuable to let him around mongrels that might have . . . fleas!

Lesson 40: "I'm always discouraged and depressed."

Examples of Behavior:

—shrugs shoulders and rolls eyes

—turns in sloppy, incomplete assignments

—tired, lack of energy

—has no confidence in decisions and answers

—procrastinates

—can't get absorbed or interested in anything

—moody, quiet, pessimistic

Reasons:

—may have physical or emotional problems

—unable to deal with situations at home, school, or among peers

—sees no purpose or reason for assignments or tasks

—has been harshly criticized for past performance

—has dealt with a lot of failure on tasks

—may have a learning disability (undetected)

Case Study:

Just being in the same room with Melissa made others feel down and depressed. Everything she said was negative and pessimistic, whether it was about the weather, the outcome of a football game, her grade on a test, or how others would react to her. It was true that she didn't have any friends; no one wanted to be around such a depressing, sad person. The school counselor talked to Melissa, and it seemed as though her home life was stable and her parents were supportive and equally concerned about her attitude. "Everything just seems pointless and hopeless," Melissa said. "You're right—I don't care about school or other people . . . or even myself. There's just no purpose for anything. We're all going to die eventually."

Things to Try:

For the student

1. Find a purpose for things. It may be as basic as enjoying something, helping someone else, appreciating beauty, etc.
2. Don't be self-centered. Look for ways to enhance someone else's life (walk through a hospital or nursing home).
3. Talk to people who are committed to a purpose or cause.
4. Investigate religion.
5. Realize that many episodes of discouragement will pass. Think: Will this be important in ten years? Will it matter?
6. Identify people and resources who will respond to you realistically when you are discouraged.
7. Keep a journal periodically. Look back over what upset you and how you feel about the situation now.

For the teacher

1. Have students read biographies of people who have made contributions to the world (a famous scientist, political leader, handicapped individuals, etc.).
2. Remind students that everyone gets discouraged sometimes.
3. Help students determine how they will choose to react to their times of discouragement (take a walk, talk to someone, get a good night's sleep, etc.).

For the parent

1. Take your child for a thorough medical exam if this condition persists.
2. Keep in close contact with your child's teacher or counselor.
3. Keep lines of communication open if your child needs to talk to you; don't be judgmental—listen.
4. If your child is using depression to be manipulative, be careful not to inadvertently reinforce this behavior (giving too much attention to negative behavior).
5. Try to identify a specific reason for the depression or discouragement. (Is it school-related? Breakup with a boyfriend? etc.)
6. Try to structure a safe, nurturing home environment—regular, healthy meals; time to spend with your child; place to do homework; get to bed at a reasonable time; etc.
7. Share your purpose in life and values with your child.
8. Enlarge your family's horizons—go to an art exhibit, get involved in a community project, start recycling. Show your child how people need, help, and appreciate each other.

Activity #1: Case Study

Have students use Worksheet #41, "Battle Plan," to come up with ideas that may help Melissa feel more optimistic about life.

Activity #2: Personal Application

Using Worksheet #41, have students work through the questions to come up with ideas to help themselves if this is a problem area for them.

Activity #3: Worksheet #61, Are You an Optimist, Pessimist, or Realist?

Synopsis: The way we view a given situation may be colored by our tendency to be optimistic or pessimistic. A brief, informal survey may help students think about how they view life.

Directions: Students are to respond to an informal survey about how they would respond to a given situation. Tabulating the results at the end will yield a score that may identify the student as an optimist, pessimist, or realist.

Discussion Questions:

1. Did the results surprise you in any way? Did you think you were primarily an optimist/pessimist/realist before you took the quiz?
2. Is it better to be one type of person than another? For example, would everyone agree that being an optimist is the best personality trait? Does optimist = good, pessimist = bad?

Journal-Entry Ideas

- Do you think of yourself as an optimist, pessimist, or realist? Why?
- When you think of a person who best describes an optimist, pessimist, and a realist, who come to mind? Why?
- What makes you feel discouraged or depressed? Do you feel you have any control over these situations?

Name____________________ Date __________

Are You an Optimist, Pessimist, or Realist? Worksheet #61

Directions: What would you do in the following situations? Circle your response to each question, then check your score at the bottom for a very **informal** rating of yourself!

1. It's been raining all week. You . . .
   (a) take the time to curl up with a good book.
   (b) go outside with an umbrella and take a nature walk through the park.
   (c) complain that you can't do anything outside and watch the weather report.

2. You just turned in your history test that you forgot to study for. You . . .
   (a) decide that graduating is not all that important.
   (b) begin planning your extra credit assignments.
   (c) won't worry about it until you get your grade.
3. Your work schedule was cut back by several hours a week. You had planned on using the money towards a new car. You. . .
   (a) decide to clean up your bicycle since you surely won't be driving anything soon!
   (b) are excited about having more time to watch television.
   (c) begin looking for a job that pays better or has more hours.
4. You see the person you have been dating for the past few weeks laughing and walking with your best friend. You . . .
   (a) intend to give this person a friendly call on the phone tonight and catch up on what's going on.
   (b) call your best friend and threaten to tell his/her secrets to the world.
   (c) are sure they are talking about what a great person you are.
5. You fell during soccer practice and your knee is swollen, black and blue, and throbbing. You . . .
   (a) continue to play anyway. You're tough!
   (b) ask the coach if he would kindly dial 9-1-1 and get an ambulance on the way.
   (c) hobble over to the nurse and ask for a quick inspection.

Scoring:

Add up your points according to the following scale:

1. a = 3 points b = 2 points c = 1 point
2. a = 1 point b = 2 points c = 3 points
3. a = 1 point b = 3 points c = 2 points
4. a = 2 points b = 1 point c = 3 points
5. a = 3 points b = 1 point c = 2 points

Total Score:

13-15 points: You are very much an optimist. You see the good side of things, even if it is a little far-fetched. You are able to put aside your worries to enjoy life.

8-12 points: You have both optimistic and pessimistic characteristics; in other words—you are a realist. You can size up a situation and make a good decision about what to do.

5-7 points: Are things really that bad? You tend to see the bleakest possible outcome of situations that maybe even haven't come to pass yet. Lighten up—things can change! Maybe you can even make them change.

Part IV

Building a Healthy Self-Esteem

The final section includes twenty-two lessons and companion worksheets that provide plenty of opportunities for developing the characteristics of healthy, successful people. Students learn to recognize these characteristics and how to make them a part of their own lifestyles.

Lesson 41: Taking Another Personal Inventory

This inventory presents students with statements that are of a positive nature. By recognizing the statements that he/she makes or hears about him-/herself, the student can hopefully realize that there is already a basis for a strong self-esteem.

Objective

- The student will complete a personal inventory in which he or she selects statements that reflect areas of high self-esteem.

Introduction

1. Have students complete the following sentences:

   I am really happy when . . .

   I like to . . .

   One of my favorite things to do is . . .

   It makes me feel proud of myself when . . .

   If I need help, I know I can count on . . .

2. Ask students to volunteer their responses if they choose. Conclude that although the statements will vary among students, there are good, positive moments and experiences in everyone's life. Taking the time to reflect upon them is not only an uplifting experience, it is also a time to realize the resources that one has.

Worksheet #62: Another Personal Inventory

Synopsis: By completing an inventory primarily dealing with positive self-statements, the student can begin to identify strengths and positive areas in his/her life.

Directions: Students are to complete the inventory and put a check mark in front of the comments they feel often describe themselves. They should write an "S" in front of those statements that sometimes describe them.

Discussion Questions:

1. Did completing this inventory make you realize how many good experiences and resources you have?
2. Do most of your good experiences have to deal with other people, experiences, talents and skills, or attitude?
3. Have any of your positive experiences happened recently, such as in the past year?

Lesson Review

1. List two or three self-statements that reflect your feelings about yourself on a usual basis.
2. List two or three self-statements that reflect your feelings about yourself on an occasional basis.

Journal-Entry Ideas

- Would you describe yourself as basically a "positive" person? Would others describe you this way also?
- How did taking the inventory make you feel? Did you feel you have a strong self-esteem or did it point out areas that you feel badly about?
- What do you think is your greatest strength?

Teacher Journal

Do you make positive statements about yourself because you feel you need to in order to be a good example to your students? What comments do you make about yourself in front of others that may not be entirely true, but you wish they were?

Name________________________________ Date __________

Another Personal Inventory

Worksheet #6.

Directions: Put a check mark in front of each statement below that you feel describes yourself o is a comment you **often** make about yourself. Put an "S" if this describes you **sometimes.**

_____ 1. I realize that I have choices in most situations.

_____ 2. I am confident about my decisions.

_____ 3. I have a lot of respect for myself.

_____ 4. I have some qualities that are unique or special.

_____ 5. There are a lot of good things about me.

_____ 6. If there is something bothering me, I can talk about it with someone else.

_____ 7. I have respect for other people.

_____ 8. When I am feeling down about something, I can usually trust myself to work it out.

_____ 9. I stand up for myself when I know I am right.

_____ 10. I have a positive attitude about life and myself.

_____ 11. I live a healthy lifestyle; I don't do things that are bad for me.

_____ 12. I listen to others when they have something to tell me.

_____ 13. I know I am not perfect and that there are some things I can't change about myself or my life.

_____ 14. I like to learn new things or try new things.

_____ 15. When others try to tell me things about myself to help me, I listen to what they have to say.

_____ 16. Sometimes I do things just because I know they are good for me.

_____ 17. I have dreams and plans for the future.

_____ 18. I'm not afraid to take risks if I know it will help me.

_____ 19. I know I can make changes in myself, others, and the world to make things better.

_____ 20. I can laugh at myself.

Lesson 42: A Foundation of Strengths

Most people have at least some idea of some personal strengths that contribute to their self-esteem. By identifying these strengths and realizing the connection of these strengths to a strong self-esteem, the individual has the makings of a foundation for further growth in the area of self-esteem.

Objective

- The student will identify several personal areas of strength that have contributed to a present self-esteem.

Introduction

Make a quick drawing of a brick building on the board. Point to the bottom bricks and ask students what would happen if those bricks were suddenly removed. *(The building would begin to collapse.)* Discuss why it is important to have a good foundation.

WORKSHEET #63: BUILDING STRENGTHS

Synopsis: There are many areas from which an individual can draw to build a good self-esteem. As people think about their past and take inventory of present skills and situations, they may realize there are certain factors that contribute to having a healthy self-esteem.

Directions: Students are to consider the questions on the worksheet which highlight several factors contributing to the development of a healthy self-esteem. They are to think of examples from their own lives that might explain how or why they have a strong self-esteem in a given area.

Discussion Questions:

1. Was it easy to think of specific examples for some of the questions?
2. Would a "good example" of someone necessarily have to be someone in a family or even someone presently living? How could another person be used as a good example?
3. How could a tragic event—such as cancer, loss of a job or home, or even death—lead to positive outcomes?
4. If no one ever told you that you are unique in some way, would you be able to figure it out yourself by comparing yourself to other people? Is it necessary to be specifically told that you are unique?
5. What decisions have you consciously made recently based upon a value that you believe in?
6. Can you think of an example in which the passage of time alone caused changes in your (or someone else's) life?

LESSON REVIEW

1. List two or three factors that personally have contributed to your strong self-esteem.
2. Explain how those factors have affected your self-esteem.

JOURNAL-ENTRY IDEAS

- Who has served as a powerful, positive example to you? In what way?
- What was "life's lesson" to you from a dramatic event in your life?
- What is the most unique or meaningful experience you have had in your life?
- If you had to pick only one value that characterized what you believe about life, what would it be? "I know for sure and believe with my whole heart that . . ."
- When did you feel you had complete and utter power over something or someone?
- Do you consider yourself to be open-minded? What is the last thing you consciously remember changing your mind about, based on new information?
- What is hard for you to wait for? In one year from now, if you did nothing, what things about life would change without any input from you?

TEACHER JOURNAL

Think of an episode in which you were totally conscious of affecting someone else—their thoughts, actions, or attitudes. What did YOU do? How did that power make you feel? Was it a positive outcome?

Name________________________________ Date ______________

Building Strengths

Worksheet #63

Directions: Below are some questions to ask yourself (and answer for yourself!) that might help you realize the strengths available to you. Think of these as building blocks to a strong, healthy self-esteem. Answer the following questions with examples or incidents from your own experience.

How might these factors help you develop a good self-esteem?

1. *A good example*
   Is there someone who inspires you, motivates you, has spent (or is willing to spend) time with you?

   ____

2. *Learning from "life lessons"*
   Have you had an experience in which you learned how to deal with someone or something or gained knowledge about something? Are you open for learning something?

   ____

3. *A unique experience*
   Have you had the opportunity to go somewhere, experience something interesting, or share something with another person that has left you better for the experience?

   ____

4. *Values—strong and clear*
   Do you have a good understanding of right and wrong, how to deal with other people, and respect for yourself? Who or what has been responsible (directly or indirectly) for helping you establish these values?

   ____

5. *Realizing you have POWER*
   Have you actively made a decision, followed through, and caused something to change for the better—directly as a result of what YOU did?

   ____

6. *An open mind*
   Are you willing to consider new information, listen to another person's opinion or viewpoint, and possibly admit that you need to change your feelings, attitude, or facts about something? This is called maturity!

   ____

7. *Time—can be your friend*
   Can you wait? Do you believe some positive changes will occur simply by letting time pass, allowing things to change, grow, mature, and become more finished or complete without your help or interference?

   ____

Lesson 43: "I realize I have choices."

Examples of Behavior:

—does not jump at the first idea presented

—takes time to consider alternative possibilities

—actively looks around for other options

—creates options; goes beyond face value

—is aware of the range of possibilities

Desired Outcome:

When placed in a situation in which the student must make a decision, he/she will identify obvious choices, realize there may be more subtle options, and expand his/her vision to include a broad range of possible choice options.

Case Study:

Danshee had a huge semester exam in biology coming up. Most of her semester grade would be based upon this exam, which was now just two weeks away. She looked at her calendar. "Oh, no," she cried, "I'm just too busy. There are two football games, a choir rehearsal and performance, a couple of piano lessons, and some Christmas shopping that I had planned to do. I don't know how I'm going to get everything in. I'll just have to cancel my piano lessons and forget about going to any football games." Her friend, Kailee, suggested she try something else. "You've got two whole weeks," she reminded her. "I bet if you planned your study time carefully, you'd be able to get everything in. Besides, I'm counting on you going shopping with me." Danshee got out her class assignment sheet and a calendar for the month. She shook her head. "I don't know . . . I don't know if I can get everything done and still do well on the test. Plus all of my other assignments!" Danshee talked it over with her piano teacher and they agreed to put off the lessons for a few weeks. She decided to go to only one football game, and spend one afternoon shopping. She also decided to make sure she had at least an hour a day to spend studying for the test.

Things to Try:

For the student

1. A "choice" implies at least two courses of actions—identify them.
2. Spend some time brainstorming about your options. What less obvious choices might you have?
3. Prioritize your time, actions, events. What is most important?
4. There may be choices, but some may not be at all helpful. Think through the potential outcomes of each choice.

For the teacher

1. Instead of spelling out the choices for students, ask them what they see as their choices.
2. Create some options as far as assignments, due dates, etc.
3. Encourage students to stick with their choices; don't waffle back and forth.
4. Check with students to see how their perception of their choice came out. Was it a mistake or a good choice?

For the parent

1. When assigning tasks for your child to do at home, allow some choice (within the realm of possibility). Not everyone hates putting clothes into the dryer or sweeping; maybe your child would better accomplish a few tasks that he/she does well than one that is continually put off or fought over.
2. Allow your child to make decisions about the order of tasks that must be done Focus on the outcome—give a time limit and just check at the end.
3. Praise your child for showing maturity and responsibility by making good choices.

Activity #1: Case Study

Have students think about the choices that Danshee had to make. Do they agree with what she decided to do? What other options did Danshee have?

Activity #2: Personal Application

Have students use Worksheet #63, "Building Strengths," to think about ways they could envision their choices in situations.

Activity #3: Worksheet #64, You Have a Choice!

Synopsis: Many situations in life involve choices of relatively equal importance. If you're going to get a pet, should it be a dog, cat, bird, or fish? To make that choice, one would have to consider room, cost, allergies, and amount of affection required. There are other types of pets, too, that perhaps should be considered—what about an iguana, ferret, or pygmy hedgehog? By expanding the possibilities, more choices become evident.

Directions: Students are to make a choice in each given situation by selecting an item from either column A or B. In most cases, the choices are simply based on personal interest—there is no right or wrong. But the items selected may tell a person something about their interests and priorities.

Discussion Questions:

1. Add Column C to each situation. What other example could you use on this worksheet?
2. What are some situations you can think of for which there is no choice? Are some choices extremely obvious? What?
3. How can someone create or invent more choices? Does negotiating with someone else create a "middle ground"?

Journal-Entry Ideas

- List at least ten choices you have had to make today. How important were these choices?
- Have you ever been in a situation in which you couldn't choose between two good things? What?
- Have you ever been in a situation in which your choices all seemed awful? How did you eventually make your decision?

Name________________________________ Date ____________

You Have a Choice!

Worksheet #64

Directions: Circle one item from Column A or Column B. You must choose one! What do your choices tell you about yourself?

	A	B
1. You can have a pet.	a lizard	a kitten
2. You have tickets for a sports event. Who will you take with you?	your best friend	your father
3. You get to pick dessert.	strawberry-topped cheesecake	an ice cream cone
4. You won a prize in a contest.	$1,000 cash	a two-week trip to Florida
5. It's Friday night and you're ready for fun.	read a good book	go to a party
6. You're getting some new clothes.	designer jeans	a sweatshirt
7. You must do a report on a famous person.	the U.S. President	a sports hero
8. You're shopping for a gift for your mother.	her favorite perfume	flowers
9. You're going to the movies.	a mystery thriller	a comedy
10. It's Saturday morning and there is nothing you have to do!	sleep in	get up and watch TV

Lesson 44: "I know how to make good decisions."

Examples of Behavior:

—considers alternatives of choices

—realizes there are choices

—thinks carefully before deciding

—uses common sense

—learns from experience

—considers information from others

—has a clear understanding of the situation

—makes choices that will lead to positive outcomes

I will carefully consider all qualified applicants for student council—and let you know my decision.
Eeny, meeny, miney, mo . . .

Desired Outcome:

When the student is in a situation involving choices, he or she will make an appropriate decision based on gathering and evaluating information, thinking through to ultimate outcomes, and desiring a positive experience.

Case Study:

Robert wasn't sure whether or not he should take World History for summer school in high school. He needed the class to graduate, but he also had the opportunity to work at his uncle's boat shop during the summer, which was a lot of fun for him and also paid well. If he took the summer school class, he would have no trouble graduating on time and would be able to take a science class in the fall that usually met at the same time as World History. What to do? Robert talked to two friends who had taken the class and found out that the course requirements were a lot easier in the summer than as a semester course. Although he would be spending half a day in school, the class only lasted five weeks so he would have time to spend working. He decided to take the class in the summer and work part-time for his uncle. It was not particularly fun going to school in the summer for Robert, but once the class was over it opened up more choices in scheduling for the fall.

Things to Try:

For the student

1. Make a pro/con sheet for each decisions. Write the good and bad possibilities of each decision.
2. Talk to people who have been in similar situations.
3. Be open-minded; don't make your decision quickly—get all the information you can.
4. Trust yourself; don't keep second-guessing your choices.

For the teacher

1. Allow your students to make their own decisions; don't be too quick to plan out everything for them.
2. Encourage students to talk to each other.
3. Expose students to conflict situations; discuss alternatives.
4. Teach students to think through a situation to a possible, logical outcome.
5. Remind students of good decisions they had made previously.

For the parent

1. Know when to become involved in the decision-making process; don't let your child fall apart, but give him/her some space.
2. If your child is thinking of becoming involved in a dangerous situation, get involved!
3. Ask questions to help direct your child's thinking. What else could happen? What might happen if you did this? Who could you talk to?
4. Some decisions are not crucial or are reversible—consider this aspect of each decision.

Activity #1: Case Study

Discuss the case study with students. How did Robert arrive at his decisions? What helped him make his decision? Did it turn out well for him? What if he had decided to work instead of going to school? Could he still have achieved the ultimate goal—to finish high school?

Activity #2: Personal Application

Use Worksheet #63, "Building Strengths," to help students think through areas that will help them make decisions if this is an area of concern for students.

Activity #3: Worksheet #65, What Would You Do?

Synopsis: Students are given the opportunity to work out possible decisions for given situations. Sometimes it helps to work with a partner or in a small group to talk through ideas.

Directions: Students are to consider the situations on the worksheet and make a decision about what to do. They are given the opportunity to obtain further information about each situation if they desire. This information should be kept separate from students until it is requested. Several groups may arrive at their decisions using entirely different patterns of thought or use of information. To vary the task, you may want to tell groups that they can only choose *one* piece of additional information; thus, they must carefully consider which piece is most crucial. You may want to assign several groups to consider only one situation at a time.

Discussion Questions:

1. Do you think you (or your group) could have made a good enough decision based on the original information or was additional information important?
2. What other questions could you have asked about the various situations?
3. Which situations were the hardest to make a decision for?
4. Which situations involved getting information or ideas from other people?
5. Which situations might have been resolved given enough *time*?
6. Which situations involved a value judgment? Would someone else who had a different value system have viewed the situation very differently?

Journal-Entry Ideas

- What is the hardest decision you ever had to make? How did it turn out?
- What is the biggest decision facing you right now? What thoughts do you have about this decision?
- How will you know if you have made the right decision? What people, events, or situations will confirm your decision?

Name________________________________ Date ____________

What Would You Do?

Worksheet #65

Directions: Below are some situations for which a decision needs to be made. By yourself, with a partner, or in a small group, come to a decision for each situation. If you want more information about some aspect of the situation, you can choose ONE piece of information to help you make a decision.

Situation #1

You really want to go to a party at the friend of a friend's house. You don't know this person very well, but you have heard the parties there are a lot of fun. Your parents, however, tell you they have heard that the police were called to the last party and that there were drugs, alcohol, and a lot of loud music. You really want to go, but don't want to be hassled by your parents. What are you going to do?

a. Do you want more information about the friend?

b. Do you want to verify what your parents have heard?

Situation #2

Your favorite grandfather, your dear old pal, has Alzheimer's disease. He lives alone, but soon he will need much more care and supervision than he has now. Your mother suggested he come to stay with your family—and share your bedroom. Although you love your grandfather, you aren't sure you want to give up half of your room. Besides that, how will living with a person with this disease affect your life? What are you going to do?

a. Do you want more information about Alzheimer's disease?

b. Do you want to know if there are alternatives to sharing your bedroom?

c. Do you want to know the present condition of your grandfather?

d. Do you want to know what your grandfather wants to do?

Situation #3

Roscoe, your dog, was hit by a car and hurt badly. It will cost a lot of money to have an operation that may help him, but he might die on the operating table. You will have to pay for his medical treatment.

a. Do you want to know how much the surgery will cost?

b. Do you want to know what's involved in taking care of the dog after surgery?

c. Do you want to know how much money you have?

d. Do you want to know more about the dog? (age, breed, etc.)

Situation #4

You are presently working at Video World as a cashier for minimum wage. The work is not hard and you get to watch movies all the time, but you are not making much money and there doesn't seem to much chance for advancement. A friend tells you about a job opening at Speedee Burgers. It seems that if you work there at minimum wage for six months, you can keep getting promoted and can become a manager and make a lot more money. The work is harder, and you have heard that the supervisor really has a bad temper, but the situation sure sounds good. What will you do?

a. Do you want to know what your supervisor at Video World would say if you asked for a raise?

b. Do you want to verify what the supervisor at Speedee Burger is like?

c. Do you want to know more about the duties at Speedee Burger?

Situation #5

Everyone in your history class is taking the final exam. Your teacher warned the class that if anyone is involved in cheating in any way, he or she will receive an "F" for the course and be referred to the principal for possible expulsion. During the test the girl who sits across from you tries to ask you for an answer to one of the questions while the teacher has his back turned. You cover your paper and shake your head, but the teacher turns around right at that moment and accuses you of cheating! Off you go to the office. What will you do?

a. Do you want to know what the principal will say to you?

b. Do you want to know what the girl who wanted to cheat will say to the principal?

c. Do you want to know your previous reputation and record in the class and at school?

Situation #6

You met a new person at a party after a football game and he/she seemed really nice. It is easy to strike up a conversation, but before you know it, the house is dark and people are starting to form couples and disappear into the house. Your new friend asks if you want to go somewhere and get to know each other a little better. You're attracted, but . . . you don't really know this person. What will you do?

a. Do you want to know the reputation of your new friend?

b. Do you want to know the truth about the habits of your new friend?

Situation #7

You purchased a slightly used bicycle from a sporting goods shop in town. The bike appeared to be in good shape and you got it for a good price. The next day, a boy comes up to you and insists that it is his bike. He said that it was stolen from his back yard about two weeks ago and that he reported it to the police. He insists that he can identify the bike because his initials are scratched under the seat. You look, but that part of the bike has been repainted, although you can see that there are scratches in the area. He says he wants his bike back.

a. Do you want to know if the boy really filed a police report?

b. Do you want to know where the sporting goods shop got the bike?

c. Do you want to know how much he is willing to pay for the bike?

d. Do you want to know if there are other bikes available at the sporting goods shop?

Further Information for Worksheet #65

Situation #1

a. The friend, a good student at a nearby high school, comes from a wealthy family and often has parties at the house for friends. They have a game room, a swimming pool, and tennis courts. The student is a member of several sports teams, is a leader in the school, and attends a church youth group regularly.

b. What your parents heard was true. The police were recently called to the house because the neighbors were disturbed by the noise. However, the party at that time was given by the parents. The neighbor who called was not invited to the party and was upset more about that than about the noise.

Situation #2

a. Alzheimer's disease affects people's ability to function. They experience severe memory loss and eventually, as the disease progresses, cannot be left alone.

b. Your father is willing to build an additional bedroom on the house, but it will take about eight months before it is finished. In the meantime, you would have to share your bedroom.

c. Presently, your grandfather only experiences memory loss and disorientation occasionally. Most of the time he is coherent and able to take care of himself.

d. Your grandfather does not want to be a burden to anyone. He is financially well-off and is willing to live in a nursing home if that is the best alternative.

Situation #3

a. The surgery is very expensive—about $500. The medicine required afterwards will be about $200.

b. Your dog will have casts on both hind legs for several weeks after the surgery. In addition, he has internal damage and will require a lot of attention. He probably won't be able to walk by himself.

c. You only work part-time and have no savings account.

d. Roscoe is a mixed breed that you picked up from the animal shelter. He weighs about 10 pounds and is 8 years old.

Situation #4

a. The supervisor would say they are unable to pay you more than minimum wage.

b. The supervisor at Speedee Burger expects a lot out of his employees and is a tough, outspoken person; however, he is very fair and will reward good workers by promotions, more choice of hours and days to work, and good recommendations to the main supervisor.

c. The duties at Speedee Burger are: coming in early to open, staying late to close, cleaning up the cooking area, waiting on customers, and keeping the salad bar full.

Situation #5

a. The principal will say he is very surprised at this situation and would like to know what you have to say before any decision is made. He also intends to talk to the girl and two witnesses in your class who have come forward on your behalf.

b. She will say you are the one who wanted her answers on the test.

c. You have never been in trouble at school before and your grades have always been above average. Most of your teachers think you are a good student and like you.

Situation #6

a. People say your new friend hangs out with gang members and has a police record a mile long. They also say this person doesn't stay long with one girlfriend/boyfriend—he/she is always on the move.

b. Your new friend has a police record that is quite long. This friend is currently on probation for theft and must report to the juvenile court next week for other charges. Your new friend seems to be really friendly, but doesn't think twice about using other people.

Situation #7

a. The boy did report a stolen bike to the police.

b. The sporting goods store got the bike in a shipment of used bikes from another state.

c. The boy is willing to pay you the same amount of money you paid to the bike shop for the bike.

d. The bike shop only has two other used bikes—a pink one with streamers coming from the handlebars and a tricycle.

Lesson 45: "I have respect for myself."

Examples of Behavior:

—speaks of self in positive terms

—does not allow others to belittle or berate him-/herself

—does not intentionally do things that are harmful to self

—takes care of self physically

—is proud of accomplishments

—is consistent with values

Desired Outcome:

The student will make choices and become involved in activities that enhance his/her abilities, are positive in nature, and demonstrate that he/she is proud of who or what he/she is and serve to improve or enhance that image.

Case Study:

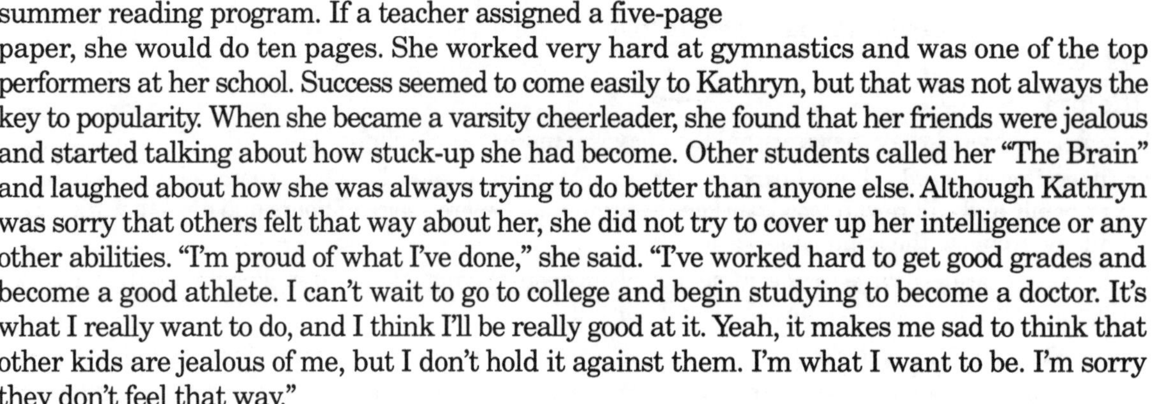

Kathryn always set high standards for herself, whether it was in school, sports, or even leisure activities. As a child, she read three times the number of books required in the summer reading program. If a teacher assigned a five-page paper, she would do ten pages. She worked very hard at gymnastics and was one of the top performers at her school. Success seemed to come easily to Kathryn, but that was not always the key to popularity. When she became a varsity cheerleader, she found that her friends were jealous and started talking about how stuck-up she had become. Other students called her "The Brain" and laughed about how she was always trying to do better than anyone else. Although Kathryn was sorry that others felt that way about her, she did not try to cover up her intelligence or any other abilities. "I'm proud of what I've done," she said. "I've worked hard to get good grades and become a good athlete. I can't wait to go to college and begin studying to become a doctor. It's what I really want to do, and I think I'll be really good at it. Yeah, it makes me sad to think that other kids are jealous of me, but I don't hold it against them. I'm what I want to be. I'm sorry they don't feel that way."

Things to Try:

For the student

1. Don't be afraid to show off a little. Reveal your strengths and successes to others.
2. Be clear about your goals and values. Don't let others sway you from what you truly believe and desire.
3. Find friends who are supportive of you.
4. Your actions speak louder than words. Show who you are by your actions.
5. Don't feel you always have to defend yourself to others.

For the teacher

1. Praise students' efforts and accomplishments.
2. Praise students' attitudes and outlooks.
3. Allow time in class for the teaching and discussion of what **respect** means.
4. Look for examples of students and others who show respect for themselves.

For the parent

1. Be a good role model of self-respect.
2. Be conscious of teaching values to your child.
3. Be ready and available to listen and support your child if he/she has to "go against the crowd."
4. Ask your child specific ways in which he/she shows respect for him-/herself.

Activity #1: Case Study

Have students listen to and discuss the case study. How does Kathryn feel about herself? How does the opinion of others make her feel? Would you advise Kathryn to do anything differently?

Activity #2: Personal Application

Have students use Worksheet #63, "Building Strengths," to think of ways in which they could improve the respect they feel for themselves.

Activity #3: Worksheet #66, Respecting Yourself

Synopsis: Respect for oneself can be experienced in many ways—it may be through comments, activities, or a general attitude about self and life. On the other hand, a lack of respect for self can show up in sloppiness, unhealthy activities, and a negative attitude.

Directions: Students are to read the examples of people who could improve their respect for themselves. They are to identify at least one way that the individual could improve his/her self-respect.

Answers (examples):

1. give up smoking; 2. don't be negative about his work; 3. decide if she wants a part in this activity; 4. get help instead of making jokes; 5. wear clean clothes, get up a little earlier; 6. do good work at all times; 7. be a person who doesn't treat others in such a way; 8. find something else to get involved in.

Discussion Questions:

1. How does respecting yourself affect taking care of your body or physical self?
2. How does respecting yourself affect your values, or what you think is important?
3. How does respecting yourself affect how others might think of you?

Journal-Entry Ideas

- Who is someone who really seems to have a lot of self-respect? What evidence makes you think this about this person?
- Do you feel you have a lot of respect for yourself? At what times do you feel strongly about this?
- Have you ever done anything for which you were really sorry later, and felt badly that you had done something that you normally would not dream of doing? Why is it so hard to stop yourself when you're right in the middle of something that you know you will be sorry for later?

Name______________________________ Date ____________

Respecting Yourself

Worksheet #6

Directions: What could each individual below do to show more respect for himself or herself?

1. Andrea wants to be an athlete. She exercises daily, eats right, and smokes cigarettes.

____

2. David is very artistic. He spends a lot of time sketching, painting, and working with clay. Wh someone came up and showed some interest in his work, he said, "Oh, this is nothing. This is ju a bunch of garbage," and tossed it aside.

____

3. Faye went shopping with a bunch of her friends. One of them thought it would be fun to shopli some earrings from a jewelry store. Faye was wearing a jacket with some big pockets in the fron Faye did not want to steal anything, but the others asked her if she would just hold their earrin in her pockets.

____

4. Marcos had trouble with an assignment in science. He knew that he was smart enough to figu it out, but sometimes he felt as though the teacher wasn't willing to help him. When he got an on his quiz, Marcos laughed and made jokes about being a rocket scientist.

____

5. Kareena rushes to get ready for her job in the morning. She usually grabs anything she can fin to put on and doesn't bother to check if it is clean or not.

____

6. Neil's father asked him to paint the garage one weekend. This was a boring job for Neil, who would rather be riding his bike or swimming, so he really didn't have his heart in it. He got paint on the windows of the garage and the sides were streaked from uneven painting. "It's just a garage," Neil argued. "No one is even going to see it up close."

____

7. Miriam wanted a date for the football game on Saturday night, but all of her usual boyfrienc were busy. She managed to get a date with Mike, a guy she really didn't like, but she knew he wa interested in her. At the last minute, another boy called her and she broke her date with Mik She heard that Mike found out what was going on.

____

8. Chuck was depressed because he didn't make the football team. He decided to go drinking with some other boys who didn't make the team. They ended up talking about how the coach played favorites and hoped that their team would have a losing season.

____

Lesson 46: "I am unique."

Examples of Behavior:

—enjoys being different

—does not apologize for eccentricities

—takes pride in accomplishments and achievements

—recognizes that he/she has unusual abilities or characteristics

—appreciates uniqueness in others

—sees things in a different way; has new perspective

—is creative

They're all trying to be unique—in the same way!

Desired Outcome:

The student will realize he/she possesses some characteristics that are unique and special, and that these characteristics are not only part of what makes him/her an individual, but may be desired and admired by others.

Case Study:

Sherman had a knack for taking something ordinary and turning it into something wild, interesting, and fun. When his neighborhood wanted to have a block party, Sherman was the one who was selling raffle tickets to help the library, organizing a pet show, and getting the neighbors enthused about the possibility of fixing up an old house that needed a lot of repairs. When sent to the store to get a gallon of milk, Sherman came home with all kinds of ingredients to make an exotic dessert—and forgot the milk. You never knew what he would bring home. After the third stray dog, his father insisted absolutely no more pets. But while Sherman was extremely kind-hearted and enthusiastic about anything he did, he was often side-tracked. Homework would be forgotten for a quick game of touch football, chores would be neglected while Sherman built a treehouse for the kids next door, and instead of typing a report on his computer, he would get the highest score ever on a computer game. Still, everyone thought the same thing: no matter what Sherman ended up doing in life, he would be great at it and would have a good time doing it.

Things to Try:

For the student

1. Be aware of how you are different from others.
2. Don't apologize for differences that are truly part of you.
3. Use your unique abilities to improve yourself.
4. Enjoy yourself—you are special!
5. Share your uniqueness with others.

For the teacher

1. Be sure to tell your students what you observe about them; how they are unique.
2. Point out uniqueness in a pleasant way ("I know George will have an unusual answer for this one. Let's hear it.").
3. Study some creative, unusual individuals (Walt Disney, Thomas Edison, etc.).
4. Allow students to work on projects that will reflect their unique perspective.
5. Encourage divergent thinking and problem solving.

For the parent

1. Siblings can be different; be careful not to compare them negatively.
2. Emphasize family pride.
3. Take photographs from time to time; these will be priceless later!
4. Make a bulletin board for each child. Let him/her fill it up with drawings, pictures, mementos of events, etc. This will make a good conversation piece for visitors.

Activity #1: Case Study

Have students think about the uniqueness of Sherman. In what ways are his qualities likeable and fun? How could his perspective on life get him into trouble? Most important, how does Sherman feel about himself?

Activity #2: Personal Application

Have students focus on their own specialness by using Worksheet #63, "Building Strengths," to recognize ways in which they are unique.

Activity #3: Worksheet #67, What Makes Us Special

Synopsis: Everyone has interesting qualities or experiences. By taking the time to get to know another person, these unique attributes become more apparent.

Directions: Students are to participate in a class activity in which they try to find another student who fits each short description on the worksheet. (The specific descriptions can and perhaps should be changed to fit the members of your class.) They are to have that student sign his/her name in each square.

Discussion Questions:

1. What did you learn about someone in your class that you were not aware of before?
2. Could you identify **one** thing about every member of your class that is unique to that person, and that person ONLY? This may take some time, but you can devise a way to single out at least one characteristic that is unique about each person.
3. Going further, could you identify one obvious characteristic about each member of the class (e.g., basketball star) and one less obvious characteristic (e.g., collects magnets from every state)?
4. How does knowing something special about a person make you feel about that person? Do you feel closer to him/her?

Journal-Entry Ideas

- What is something about yourself you wish others knew?
- Have you had the opportunity to go somewhere or experience something that is somewhat unusual? Write about it. How did this affect you?
- Sometimes what makes us special is not what we've done, where we've been, or what we've accomplished, but simply the kind of person we are. Who is someone who may not be outstanding or a great achiever in any certain way, but is a "special" person? Why?

Name____ Date ______________

What Makes Us Special

Worksheet #67

Directions: This is a group activity involving interaction among members of the group. Below are some examples of unique or interesting characteristics or events involving individuals. Each member of the group should circulate around the room, getting signatures from other members in each square that pertains to that individual. Your time limit is: ________________ .

has been to another country	**loves reptiles**	**good at basketball**
favorite TV show is ________________	**has no sisters or brothers**	**could be a professional singer**
favorite candy bar is ________________	**got all A's**	**has a horse**
likes having blonde hair	**not afraid to wear bold clothes**	**collects baseball cards**
likes puppies	**won a trophy**	**met someone famous**

Lesson 47: "There are a lot of good things about me."

Examples of Behavior:

—has positive outlook on life

—can list several good attributes about self

—is objective about self

—listens to what others tell him/her

—believes in self

—not boastful, but willing to tell about accomplishments

Desired Outcome:

The student will be able to state or list several personal things about him-/herself that he/she feels represent good things about his/her self.

Case Study:

Susan is a very quiet girl, and it wasn't until a teacher discovered fantastic drawings in her math notebook that anyone was aware of her artistic ability. At first her shyness prevented her from wanting anyone to see what she could do, but as she began to realize that people were truly interested in her work, Susan began to draw sketches for other people—including a bulletin board for a teacher. Eventually she helped the art teacher as an assistant and directed the designing, drawing, and painting of a huge mural across the wall of the cafeteria. Proudly, she signed her name in the corner on the day it was finished. "I don't mean to brag," she insists, "but I love to draw and I'm so glad now that people know about this. I want to become a professional artist, and I feel that if this many people like what I can do now . . . well, just think what I'll be able to do with some professional training. I love it when people look at my work! Maybe someday I'll be famous."

Things to Try:

For the student

1. Show off what you can do (without being obnoxious, of course!).
2. Let a friend brag for you.
3. Listen to what people say about you.
4. Make a conscious effort to get a reaction from others; have them respond to something you do or something you are.
5. Decide to hang around with positive people.

For the teacher

1. Incorporate a "student of the week" into your plan; highlight each student.
2. Act like you believe everyone has something good about him/her.
3. Try harder with unpopular students; find something good in them.
4. Realize that you may have to dig a little more with quiet, private students—look for surprises.

For the parent

1. You know your child quite well—don't dwell on the imperfections that must be changed.
2. For every criticism, give a compliment.
3. Tell your child what you find interesting, fascinating, funny about him/her.
4. Ask your child periodically what he/she is learning about herself or himself; has he/she matured? point of view changed? values been challenged?

Activity #1: Case Study

Perhaps the students can relate to someone like Susan, who is very quiet about her talents. Have them think about why Susan may have been hesitant to share her abilities publicly at first. What other characteristics (other than her artistic ability) does Susan seem to have that others might find attractive?

Activity #2: Personal Application

Have students use Worksheet #63, Building Strengths, to think of ways in which they can improve their own thinking about themselves; specifically, what is good about themselves.

Activity #3: Worksheet #68, Good Things About Me

Synopsis: Everyone has good things about them. These "good" things do not necessarily have to be an accomplishment; in fact, personality traits may be even more important when evaluating ourselves. Nevertheless, time spent on thinking about our strengths is a good basis for building self-esteem.

Directions: Students are to fill in the outline of a person with comments about themselves indicating some things they feel are good about themselves.

Discussion Questions:

1. Look over what you wrote on the worksheet. How many of your comments are about things you can do? How many are about the kind of person you are? What do you think this shows about what you feel is important?
2. Did you think of specific instances of examples in which you felt you were good?
3. How important is the opinion of others when evaluating oneself?
4. Do you think there are some people who think they have some really good qualities, but everyone else would disagree with them? How could you explain this "blindness" to self?

Journal-Entry Ideas

- When was the last time someone said the word "good" to you? What was it in reference to? Something you did well? Something you said? An evaluation of a written assignment? How did it make you feel?
- Do you think people are basically good or bad? Why do you think so?
- Think of some characters that are villains in the movies, on TV, or in cartoons. What characteristics make us think of them as evil or wicked? Now, what good characteristic can you find for each of them?

Name______________________________ Date ____________

Good Things About Me

Worksheet #6

Directions: Fill in the diagram below with things you feel are good about yourself. This is your chance to show what you're made of! Feel free to write in the space around the diagram, too!

Ideas: things you've accomplished, things you've won, experiences you have had, people who are important to you, what others tell you they like about you, etc.

Lesson 48: "I can talk about my feelings."

Examples of Behavior:

—is open with others

—is able to express self in words

—is honest about how he/she feels

—trusts others with information and feelings

—does not hold questions and problems inside

—tends to ask questions (perhaps hoping for an opening)

Desired Outcome:

The student will be able to express him-/herself in words to another person, especially when the student is experiencing a problem, conflict, or questions.

Case Study:

Daniel was not coping well with his mother's remarriage—and the sudden addition of several younger stepsisters, not to mention moving to a new house and enrolling in a new school. Everything seemed to be changing for him. It would be several years before he could get a job and move out of the house, so it seemed to Daniel as though the next few years would be a time of turmoil and constant, unwelcome changes. His best friend, Mike, realized what he was going through (having been through a somewhat similar experience). They would often talk about the problems associated with having to get along with new siblings and dealing with a new adult. Since Daniel was spending so much time at Mike's house, he got to know Mike's stepfather, Alan, pretty well. One afternoon, after the three had finished playing basketball in the yard, Alan asked Daniel how things were going at home. Daniel trusted Alan, and took advantage of the opportunity to let him know of his fears and doubts about his new family situation. Alan agreed that it was hard at first, and probably would be for awhile, but that his new stepfather was no doubt having some fears as well—just as Alan had. Through their informal talks, Daniel expressed his feelings and got a new perspective on what it must be like for others besides himself to become a new family. "It's really nice to know that someone else has been through what I'm going through," he said. "Alan has become a good friend to me; I feel like I can tell him anything and he'll understand."

Things to Try:

For the student

1. Don't rule out talking to a parent, trusted adult, school counselor, etc.
2. Think about what you want to say and practice putting it in words.
3. If you are really upset, you may want to wait a little while before talking; think it through.
4. Make a mental list of some people whom you already trust and feel comfortable with.

For the teacher

1. Be available to students who may want to talk to you.
2. Stress that everyone needs to talk to someone at times; that doesn't indicate there's something "wrong" with you.
3. Make sure students are aware of trained personnel (counselor, nurse) who might be able to give advice.
4. Honor a student's request for confidentiality (unless the information must be reported to authorities); don't discuss it in the teachers' lounge, etc.

For the parent

1. Realize that you may be too close to a situation; your child may need to talk to someone who is a little more removed.
2. Give your child opportunities to verbalize what he/she is doing, thinking, etc.; make it more comfortable for him/her to put thoughts into words.
3. Go first; express a concern or problem you may be experiencing to your child and ask for an opinion or comment.

Activity #1: Case Study

Have students discuss how Daniel was able to find and use people around him to talk over his situation. Who else could Daniel have talked to? In what ways might this experience prepare Daniel to help someone else?

Activity #2: Personal Application

Using Worksheet #63, "Building Strengths," have students go through their own particular situations to look for ways they could develop the skills associated with being able to talk things over with others.

Activity #3: Worksheet #69, Talking It Over

Synopsis: Being able to put feelings into words and being willing to express those words with others is a way to help build one's self-esteem.

Directions: Students are to choose one (or more) of given situations that involve talking over a hypothetical problem with a designated individual. Students can role play the situations in front of the class.

Discussion Questions:

1. In what situations is it easier to talk to someone the same age as you?
2. In what situations might it be more helpful to talk to an adult?
3. How could talking something over change a situation?
4. What might happen if you choose the "wrong person" to confide in? Why should you be careful to trust your confidante?
5. How could someone who has not been through your exact type of problem still be able to help you?

Journal-Entry Ideas

- Keep track of your emotional ups and downs for a week. Practice putting your feelings into words on paper. What makes you upset? When did you feel extremely happy? What surprised you today?
- Who is a person whom you would trust if you needed to confide in someone? Why did you select this person?

Name____ Date ______________

Talking It Over

Worksheet #69

Directions: Choose one of the following situations. Pick a partner and take turns being the talker and the listener. Present a short skit to the class.

Situation #1:

A student is having problems getting along with a teacher. The student wants to discuss this with another teacher.

Situation #2:

A boy is interested in asking out a new girl at school, but he isn't sure how to approach her. He is talking it over with a male friend.

Situation #3:

Same situation as #2, but talking it over with a female friend.

Situation #4:

A person is afraid his/her best friend is starting to get involved with a gang. He/she is talking to a counselor.

Situation #5:

A student is concerned about his/her parents' drinking. The student is talking to an adult friend.

Situation #6:

A student is trying to decide whether to purchase a really expensive bicycle or save the money towards a used car. He/she is talking with a parent.

Situation #7:

A person wants to spend spring break in Florida with the family of a good friend, but is afraid that Mom and Dad will object. Talk it over with the good friend.

Situation #8:

Your "nerdy" cousin moves to town and is going to your school. You really don't want anyone to know that this person is related to you, but . . . this *is* your cousin and you feel a lot of family pressure. Talk to another family member.

Lesson 49: "I show respect for other people."

Examples of Behavior:

—accepts authority from adults

—is polite and courteous to older people

—does not take advantage of others

—looks for opportunities to assist others

—does not belittle others

—waits and lets others go first

Desired Outcome:

In social situations, the student will consider the needs of others first.

Case Study:

Tiaga rode the city bus to get to her aunt's house every day after school. The bus was often crowded, and sometimes people had to fight to get a seat. Every day Tiaga would notice how rude people were to the bus driver, complaining about conditions that were beyond the driver's control. She also observed how sometimes older people did not get a seat, but had to stand for long periods of time. One day she decided she was going to be different; she was going to take a stand to make a difference. First, she smiled at the bus driver, wished him a good afternoon, and then pleasantly took a seat. When an older woman got on the bus, she got up to let the woman have her seat. "That's a well-mannered young lady," she heard a woman comment to the man sitting next to her. "I wish there were more people like her."

Things to Try:

For the student

1. Decide on one thing you will do today that will show respect for someone else.
2. Spend some time observing how others interact with authority figures; find examples of showing respect and disrespect.
3. Go through a day listing people whom you encounter and should show respect to.

For the teacher

1. Have the class make a poster entitled "What Respect Looks Like/Sounds Like/Acts Like" and fill in examples.
2. List ways that individuals and the class as a whole could show respect for people at the school.
3. Set an example of being respectful to others.

For the parent

1. Model respect for others in front of your child.
2. Express dissenting opinions tactfully.
3. Ask your child to think of ways to show respect for someone you may encounter.
4. Look for examples of showing respect and lack of respect.

Activity #1: Case Study

Have students talk about ways that Tiaga showed respect to others. How did this affect observers around her? What did Tiaga gain from her actions?

Activity #2: Personal Application

Have students use Worksheet #63, "Building Strengths," to find ways they can build their own self-esteem by showing respect to others.

Activity #3: Worksheet #70, Ways to Show Respect

Synopsis: There are many individuals we encounter on a daily basis with whom we interact. It shows good character to habitually show respect to these people.

Directions: Students are to think of ways they could show respect for the individuals listed on the worksheet. They are to write down their ideas.

Discussion Questions:

1. Why is it sometimes harder to show respect to an authority figure than to a complete stranger?
2. Why should you show respect to someone who may not respond by showing respect back to you?
3. If respect means putting someone else first, how does that translate to any kind of gain for you?
4. What if an authority figure wanted you to do something that you truly disagreed with? How could you disagree and still show respect?

Journal-Entry Ideas

- Select an individual who will be your target for one week. Keep track of the ways you will go out of your way to show respect for this individual. Keep track of what happens and how it affects you and the individual.
- What is the most unpopular job or role you can think of? How could someone hold this position and still get respect from others?

Name____ Date ______________

Ways to Show Respect

Worksheet #7(

Directions: How could you show respect for the individuals listed below? Think about it and writ(e) your creative responses!

a city police officer

____

____

____

an unpopular principal

____

____

____

your best friend's mother

____

____

____

your math teacher

____

____

____

your coach

____

____

____

a handicapped student

____

____

____

the school secretary

____

____

____

the school lunch staff

____

____

____

the clerk at the drug store

____

____

____

a waitress

____

____

____

an old person walking his dog

____

____

____

a mother holding a squirming baby

____

____

____

Lesson 50: "I can trust myself to work problems out."

Examples of Behavior:

—knows strengths and skills

—does not run away from problem situations

—knows when a problem is beyond his/her ability to solve without assistance

—recognizes the seriousness of some situations

—willing and able to try problem-solving technique

Desired Outcome:

When confronted with a problem situation, the student will assess it and decide whether or not he/she can solve the problem alone or with assistance.

Case Study:

Ramon lived in a tough urban neighborhood. Crime and violence were a part of his life. Although Ramon did not want to become a part of this lifestyle, he could not help but be affected by all that was around him. His older brother had already been shot twice by drug dealers in the area. His sister dropped out of school to get a job. His father had disappeared years ago. The family was primarily held together by an overworked mother and a sickly grandmother. Through his circumstances, Ramon had become a survivor. He was able to decide on his goals and his course of action and not be sidetracked by the problems all around him. He had the strength to be able to avoid social problems that surrounded him. As he grew older, he found that he had acquired a lot of wisdom learned through hard lessons of his life. Years later, Ramon finished medical school and became a doctor. He chose to practice in a hospital in the very center of the area where he lived when he was growing up. "If anyone can relate to these people, it's me," he said. "I know what these patients are going through. Best of all, maybe now I can do something to help them. Not just physically, but mentally. I want to give them hope. They feel that there is no one they can trust. They can trust me—and they can learn to trust themselves."

Things to Try:

For the student

1. Think about some problems you have handled easily. What skills were involved in resolving them?
2. Select a challenge for yourself, something that will put your skills to the test.
3. Make an effort to raise your hand to answer a question in every class every day. Show yourself, your teacher, and others that you trust yourself to know an answer or express an opinion.
4. Think about some problems you have handled with the help of others. How did their assistance give you the resolve to work out the problem?

For the teacher

1. Occasionally question the student's responses: "Are you sure about what you just said? Do you have any evidence?" Although this can be disconcerting at first, it will teach the students that you expect them to defend themselves.
2. Tell students you trust them in given situations; give them your vote of confidence.
3. Ask students to talk about experiences in which they learned to trust their own judgment.
4. Everyone's tolerance for handling problems may differ. Point out that what is not a problem for one person may be a very severe problem for another.
5. Teach students to "be their own coach." Think of a few phrases that students can use for self-talking (e.g., "I know I can do this; I've done it before!").
6. Assign biographical reading such as *The Diary of Ann Clark;* people *do* cope!

For the parent

1. Give your child opportunities to make decisions (which may include mistakes).
2. Look for or create opportunities for your child to be trusted with responsibility.
3. Talk about why there is or is not trust between you and your child.
4. Be prepared to forgive past errors; don't hold mistakes against your child forever.
5. Ask your child periodically to assess his/her trust in him-/herself; "Can you handle this?" Do you think this will become a problem?"

Activity #1: Case Study

Even though Ramon had a lot of strikes against him as a child, he managed to make a success of himself as an adult. Unfortunately, there are too few examples of this type of success. Have the class discuss how Ramon overcame a lot of bad influences in his childhood. How much of a factor was Ramon's belief in himself? Who or what helped him along the way? Why do you think Ramon chose to return to this culture as an adult?

Activity #2: Personal Application

Some students may struggle with trusting their own judgment in life situations. Have them work through the questions on Worksheet #63, "Building Strengths," to think about areas that will help them develop strength in the area of trusting oneself.

Activity #3: Worksheet #71, Trusting Yourself

Synopsis: It is important to recognize one's own limitations. There are some areas of life that are easier for some people to deal with than others. But knowing yourself so well that you can almost predict what situations will give you problems is an important advantage in life.

Directions: Students are to complete a survey that poses examples of problems they might face at some point. They are to consider which of the items could be handled by the individual (trusting themselves to handle it successfully) and mark those with a +. Items that would require additional assistance should be marked +/–. Those items students feel are beyond their abilities, even with assistance, should be marked –.

Discussion Questions:

1. Look at the items you marked with a +. Do you know that you could handle these situations because of previous experience? prior knowledge? basic disposition or personality? Think about why you were confident enough to mark them with a +.
2. Look at the items you marked with a +/–. Why were you unsure about being able to cope with the problem? Do you have someone or something specifically in mind that would help you?
3. Did you mark any items with a – ? What do you feel is so awful or so intolerable that you could not cope? Again, is there a previous experience involved that has made you feel this way?

Journal-Entry Ideas

- Has someone ever said to you, "I don't know how you can deal with that"? What was the situation? What did someone admire about you? Maybe something seems easy for you to deal with, but only because you never thought about how difficult it might seem for someone else.
- Have you ever said, "I could never handle that situation"? What was it in reference to? Do you know of anyone who is in that particular situation right now? How do they handle it?
- People who feel they can't cope with certain situations may try desperate measures or do harmful things such as trying to commit suicide, run away, or get involved in even worse situations. What would you tell your best friend or your brother/sister if you found out this individual was seemingly unable to cope with a situation?

Name________________________________ Date ______________

Trusting Yourself

Worksheet #71

Directions: Below is a survey of some situations or problems you might face someday. How strongly do you feel about your ability to cope with each? Indicate your response by putting a number in front of each item on the list. Use the following key:

+ = "I can handle this situation; no problem!"

+/– = "I'm not completely sure I could handle this one; I might need some help or support."

– = "There is no way I could cope with that!"

Then complete the **Personal List** on page 2 with some examples of situations from your life that show varying degrees of trust in yourself.

How well would you handle . . .

______ 1. getting an F on your report card?

______ 2. being fired from a job?

______ 3. being embarrassed in front of your friends by someone you don't like?

______ 4. finding out your parents are getting a divorce?

______ 5. finding out you are pregnant/got someone pregnant?

______ 6. being approached to get involved with a gang?

______ 7. being involved in an accident in which someone is severely hurt?

______ 8. having to take care of a very sick, elderly grandparent?

______ 9. seeing your boyfriend/girlfriend with another person?

______ 10. finding out your parents lied to you about something important?

______ 11. taking the family car without permission and getting a dent in it?

______ 12. being offered a large amount of money to do something wrong?

______ 13. joining a group of friends in minor vandalism?

______ 14. lending money to someone who probably will not ever pay you back?

______ 15. lying to your parents about where you were and who you were with?

Personal List

Things I KNOW I can handle without a problem:

a. ______________________________

____

b. ______________________________

____

c. ______________________________

____

d. ______________________________

____

Things I THINK would be a problem for me:

a. ______________________________

____

b. ______________________________

____

c. ______________________________

____

d. ______________________________

____

Things I absolutely could NOT deal with on my own:

a. ______________________________

____

b. ______________________________

____

c. ______________________________

____

d. ______________________________

____

Lesson 51: "I stand up for what I believe in."

Examples of Behavior:

—has strong, well-defined beliefs or values

—is vocal about opinions

—accepts challenges to point of view

—gives reasons for beliefs

—willing to take action to support beliefs

Desired Outcome:

The student will not only defend his/her beliefs and values when confronted or questioned about them, but will actively participate in activities that promote those beliefs and values.

Case Study:

Lynette had leukemia as a child. She still remembers taking weekly trips to the children's hospital three hours away for her painful treatments. She remembers being nauseous and experiencing painful throbbing in her legs. She now can laugh at pictures of her as a young child, bald with a headband on her forehead—the only clue that she was a girl. Now, years later, the disease is under control and Lynette is leading a normal life. Still, she remembers how having this disease was painful and restrictive when she was young. Now as a high school student, she devotes several hours each week to volunteering to play with patients on the children's ward at the local hospital. She and both of her parents are on committees for promoting research to find a cure for leukemia. Occasionally she participates in fund-raising activities. "It's really hard," she says. "People don't want to give money. There are so many diseases around and this is not a popular one. And unless you know someone who's had it, you probably aren't that interested in finding out about it. But every chance I get, I tell people that I beat this disease. It's not the time to stop trying to find a cure. I'll just keep trying."

Things to Try:

For the student

1. Make a list of some concerns or beliefs you feel strongly about.
2. Look through a newspaper and try to identify some "hot issues" in your community; what is your reaction?
3. What events have been a part of your life that have affected what you feel strongly about?
4. What one thing would you like to see changed? How could you become involved?

For the teacher

1. Spend class time on awareness of community issues—look at both sides.
2. Structure an informal "debate." Research pros and cons of an issue.
3. Arrange for a speaker to talk to the class (someone who has had an interesting experience, community leader, doctor, scientist, etc.).
4. Make a list of "hot topics." Take a class survey *before* studying the issue and then *after* time has been spent studying the facts of both sides.
5. Have students design posters or bumper stickers (be creative).

For the parent

1. Join your child in his/her attempt to promote a cause (if you believe in it!).
2. Question your child as to **why** he or she believes so strongly in an issue; is it simply to follow a trend?
3. When you read an interesting or controversial news article or watch the news on TV, ask your child for his/her opinion.

Activity #1: Case Study

Have students discuss reasons why Lynette is so strongly devoted to her cause. Would she feel the same if her sister or brother had contracted the disease? What discourages Lynette about the present situation? What else could she do to promote awareness of leukemia?

Activity #2: Personal Application

Have students think about their own personal values and beliefs. Use Worksheet #63, "Building Strengths," to get some ideas about why this is an important issue and how they can promote their beliefs.

Activity #3: Worksheet #72, Take a Stand

Synopsis: By becoming actively involved in a cause, we can see for ourselves how important it is to us.

Directions: Students are to select an issue about which they feel very strongly—strongly enough to get involved in some aspect of it. They are to get involved (as much as possible or practical) and report on their success and findings.

Journal-Entry Ideas

- If you could donate $1 million privately to a charity or cause, what would it be? Would you be more likely to donate to a cause if everyone knew about it?
- What are some causes that are "close to home" for you? Who or what may have been a factor in your choice of this cause?

Name________________________________ Date ____________

Take a Stand

Worksheet #72

Directions: What is something you feel very strongly about? Look through the local newspaper . . . listen to what people are concerned about . . . walk through your community . . . and then plan to take a stand on something. Use the following ideas to get you started:

1. What is something you feel very strongly about?
2. Why do you feel so strongly about this?
3. What is a way you could make your views known about this?
4. Is there already an existing group or organization that tries to promote this idea or position?
5. Get involved. Join others or do something to let others know how you feel and then ACT upon that feeling.
6. How did it go? How did you feel? Did you make a difference to someone in any way?

Lesson 52: "I have a positive attitude about life and myself."

Examples of Behavior:

—looks at the positive side of things

—sees something good in every situation

—notices good attributes about people

—takes bad news in stride

—attempts to turn bad situations into good ones

—is willing to learn new things

—is interested in what's going on around him/her

Desired Outcome:

Given normal situations, the student will approach them in a positive manner by accepting a challenge, deciding to learn something new, and/or finding something good or positive about each situation.

Case Study:

Peter and his family moved from Poland to a small town in the Midwest. Although Peter had been a fairly good student before the move, he struggled in school in America. He had a tutor who helped him with his schoolwork and he was taking classes in English, but the language barrier was extremely frustrating for him. Peter decided to start going to the local YMCA after school just to shoot some baskets by himself. Another boy from his school noticed him and asked if he would like to join them in a game. Soon Peter found himself involved in informal basketball games with other students from his school. Peter was tall, athletic, and he had played basketball before, so it was only a matter of time until he became a regular on the court. Through basketball, Peter began to interact with the other students—and learned quite a bit of informal English! By deciding to do something he was interested in anyway, Peter made himself available to socialize with other kids. He was determined to have a good time, no matter what the circumstances were.

Things to Try:

For the student

1. When situation looks bad, give it some time—it may work itself out.
2. Decide on *one* thing you can do to make something change.
3. Get a second opinion on the situation from someone you trust.
4. Find something that is good or potentially positive about each situation.

For the teacher

1. Have the class study some famous disasters or tragedies and study the positive outcomes (e.g., *Titanic* disaster led to safety regulations).
2. When students complain about something, ask them to find something positive about the situation.
3. Challenge students to go through one complete day (class period?) with only positive comments.
4. Spend some time assessing whether or not a situation can be changed or if it has to be accepted as is.

For the parent

1. Look for examples among your friends and your child's friends of good attitudes, especially in times of conflict or adversity.
2. Choose to ignore negative comments; respond to your child when he/she is speaking positively.
3. Some unpleasant situations are beyond anyone's control; in that event, decide how you and your family will react to them.
4. Praise your child for making positive comments.
5. Acknowledge a positive attitude.
6. Help your child make a list of ten immediate things he/she/the family can do to throw off depression (e.g., take a walk, play a game, go to a movie, make a pizza, etc.).

Activity #1: Case Study

Spend some time discussing Peter's situation. While the move to America was probably not his idea, he managed to cope with it. How did his attitude towards the move affect what happened to him? What else could Peter do to make this a better, more tolerable, situation for himself?

Activity #2: Personal Application

Using Worksheet #63, "Building Strengths," have students decide on ways they can build a positive attitude towards events that are occurring in their own lives.

Activity #3: Worksheet #73, Turning Things Around

Synopsis: Every negative situation or attitude can have a positive side. It may take some thinking, but within every potentially "bad" situation is something that can be useful.

Directions: Students are to read each example of a possibly negative situation and write an example of a potentially positive outcome or helpful lesson learned.

Answers (examples):

1. It's a good day to get inside work done. 2. We'll have to try harder to win this game. 3. I'm going to set aside this evening to catch up. 4. My car should be good for a long time now after that repair! 5. I'm going to gain some new skills. 6. Think of the money! 7. I'm going to enjoy today and remember how much fun it was when I'm in school at the end of the year. 8. This running will probably make me stronger.

Discussion Questions:

1. How can there be anything positive out of a horrible tragedy?
2. Does the attitude or outlook that someone has about something affect how hard the tragedy hits?
3. Can you think of an example of someone who dealt with a negative situation in a positive way? What happened? Where did their strength come from?
4. How does it make you feel to be around people who look at the negative side of everything?
5. Do you think some people who always seem to be overly-positive are just faking it? Why would they do that?
6. Do you think some people are just born with good attitudes or can they be developed?

Journal-Entry Ideas

- List 5 to 10 things you are worried or concerned about. Next to each, write one potentially positive outcome that might occur. Is there any way you can make that happen?
- What you say is a reflection of your attitude. Resolve to say ten positive things throughout the day, despite what you have to face. Does saying something positive make you feel more positive?

Name____ Date ____________

Turning Things Around

Worksheet #73

Directions: Turn each of the following negative attitudes and statements into something positive.

1. What a dismal day. I hate rain.

____

____

2. I know our team is going to lose again.

____

____

3. Oh, no! . . . I didn't get my homework done last night. I'm already behind!

____

____

4. I can't believe my car needs $100 worth of work.

____

____

5. This new job means I have to learn a whole bunch of new things. I don't know if I'm smart enough.

____

____

6. But I don't want to babysit for my little cousin! I want to go OUT!

____

____

7. There's no school today because of snow—but we have to make it up in the summer!

____

____

8. We have to run laps in P.E. I hate running. I hate sweating!

____

____

Lesson 53: "I live a healthy lifestyle; I don't do things that are bad for me."

Examples of Behavior:

—exercises regularly; plays sports

—controls temper

—does not take drugs (alcohol, tobacco, illegal drugs)

—avoids people who don't make good decisions

—spends time with friends

—is on good terms with family

—has clear values

—balances different areas of life (physical, spiritual, academic, etc.)

—has an open mind

This started as an after-school aerobics class—but now we just breathe deeply and exchange low-fat recipes.

Desired Outcome:

The student will recognize what factors contribute to living a healthy lifestyle and refrain from engaging in things that do not promote good health.

Case Study:

Katrina had always been overweight. It seemed to be a family trend—possibly related to poor eating habits, rushing around during meals, eating a lot of fast food, and eating during times of stress...and times of pleasure. Although she hated looking in a mirror, she just could not give up eating and eating and eating. One day a friend of hers, Charlotte, encouraged her to work out at the YMCA after school with her. At first Katrina found a lot of excuses not to do it—lots of homework, too tired, too busy, etc., but eventually she agreed to give it a try. She found that there were quite a few girls from her class who used the YMCA for swimming, working out with weights, and playing basketball. After Katrina lost the first ten pounds, she started liking what she saw in the mirror. With Charlotte's encouragement, Katrina continued to exercise almost daily over the winter—and lost a total of twenty-two pounds. Her desire to eat constantly went away too. She realized how hard it was to lose even one pound, and didn't want to undo all of her hard work. Forget smoking and drinking—she was determined to keep the weight off by taking care of herself. Katrina and Charlotte decided to buy bicycles and get fresh air and exercise outside during the summer. When she returned to school in the fall, she felt good about herself—not just her looks, but the fact that she was in control of what happened to her.

Things to Try:

For the student

1. Take a quick inventory of your habits. What do you need to get rid of?
2. Find time to put exercise into your schedule. How could you do two things at once? (study on the stationary bicycle; walk the dog through a park)
3. Find a supportive friend and make a pact to start doing one thing differently.
4. Try eating foods that are supposed to be good for you—you may be pleasantly surprised!
5. Add one social activity to your life.

For the teacher

1. Invite an appropriate guest speaker (a doctor, aerobics instructor) to share experiences in healthful living. Maybe have a mini-lesson?
2. Give students *facts* about drugs and alcohol.
3. Do a lesson/demonstration on heart rate.

4. Obtain a list of what factors contribute to a long life (e.g., wearing a seat belt, family factors, avoiding tobacco, etc.).

For the parent

1. Re-think your eating habits.
2. Teach your child to look at and understand the nutrition facts on packaged food.
3. Quit smoking and drinking.
4. Get rid of the junk food in your cabinet.
5. Provide alternative activities to watching television. How about family tennis lessons?
6. Wear your seat belt; drive carefully.

Activity #1: Case Study

Katrina (with Charlotte's help) made a transformation in her life—not just physically, but in other areas as well. How did this boost her self-confidence? What do you predict for Katrina at school the next year?

Activity #2: Personal Application

Have students use Worksheet #63, "Building Strengths," to identify ways in which they could promote and begin living more of a healthy lifestyle.

Activity #3: Worksheet #74, A Healthy Lifestyle

Synopsis: Many areas contribute to an overall healthy lifestyle. These include physical, social, attitudinal, as well as values and beliefs.

Directions: Students are to give examples of ways an individual could live a healthy lifestyle given several areas of life.

Discussion Questions:

1. What are some ways to have fun that aren't physically harmful? What are some ways to have fun that would be considered risky or dangerous? Why would someone choose to have fun in that manner?
2. Do you think students are more conscious of being physically fit than parents are?
3. How can certain people be considered "harmful" to another person? On the other hand, how can others be "helpful" to promoting a healthy lifestyle?
4. Do you feel you know what is important to keep your body healthy? If not, where could you get this information?
5. What do you feel are the important things everyone needs to learn about life? Where are these things taught?

Journal-Entry Ideas

- Rate your lifestyle on a scale of 1 to 10, with 10 being the most healthy and 1 being the least healthy. Why did you rate yourself this way?
- What habits do you see in your parents or other family members that you are now aware of in yourself? How does this make you feel?

Name________________________________ Date ______________

A Healthy Lifestyle

Worksheet #74

Directions: Give examples of ways you can have a healthy lifestyle in the following areas.

ways to have fun without hurting myself or others	how to keep myself physically fit
staying away from people and things that are harmful	what everyone needs to learn about life
what is important; what is meaningful to me	people who matter to me; friends and family who are there for me

Lesson 54: "I am a good listener."

Examples of Behavior:

—does not interrupt

—asks questions about what was said

—can paraphrase what was said

—understands body language; interprets correctly

—listens without being defensive

Desired Outcome:

The student will listen carefully when another person is speaking, to the extent that the student can correctly paraphrase the speaker's message, including the intent and tone of speaker.

Case Study:

Ron's family had problems, but they were no different than anyone else's. The thing that was different in Ron's family was the way they handled problems. They sat down at the kitchen table and discussed each family item while sharing a favorite dessert. The rules were simple: the problem would be stated (usually by the person who was upset by something), both sides would be examined, and the family would all have a chance to discuss what they saw as the problem, possible solutions, and the first thing to try. "I was really mad at my sister," Ron explains. "We were supposed to be taking turns doing the dishes and taking out the trash, but it always seemed as though Sara had excuses—too much homework, a meeting after school, just plain busy—and I was always doing it. My mom would just say, 'I don't care who does it, just so it gets done. You two work it out,' but that wasn't working for us. We had to admit—we needed someone to tell us what to do." Ron's mother adds, "We finally made a chart with family chores listed. Trading is allowed, but only if both sides agree. At the end of the week, we look at it as a family and decide how well it is working. There is no screaming, no arguing—and no talking when someone else is talking." Sara's comments: "I really am too busy to do chores in the afternoon. But it works out well for me to do work in the morning or on weekends. Once Ron understood that I wasn't trying to get out of work—I was just trying to reschedule it—I think he was more willing to trade chores with me."

Things to Try:

For the student

1. Practice not interrupting.
2. Wait five seconds before you talk; collect your thoughts.
3. Try paraphrasing what the other speaker has said.
4. Ask more questions.
5. Look at the speaker in the eye.

For the teacher

1. Practice skills of summarizing and paraphrasing.
2. Ask students to paraphrase what you say (in a lecture situation).
3. Work on developing a longer attention span for listening.
4. Have students listen to television broadcasts without the picture, only sound.

For the parent

1. Sit together with your child and listen to a news show on TV or other documentary; discuss what you heard.
2. Have occasional sit-down meals together with your family; take turns conversing and listening to each other.
3. Practice restating what your child has said ("So what you mean is . . . ").
4. Ask your child what he/she has heard you say.

ACTIVITY #1: CASE STUDY

Discuss how Ron's family handled the problems affecting this family. How was lack of communication contributing to the problem of scheduling chores? How did the family work on better communication?

ACTIVITY #2: PERSONAL APPLICATION

Most students could probably benefit from improving their listening skills. Use the ideas on Worksheet #63, "Building Strengths," to work on improving this skill.

ACTIVITY #3: WORKSHEET #75, WHAT DO YOU HEAR?

Synopsis: By consciously listening to someone else, an individual can practice tuning in to the message that the speaker wants to convey.

Directions: Students are to select several individuals listed on the worksheet (although others could certainly be substituted) and spend at least five minutes consciously listening to them speak. The student may ask questions to keep the conversation going, if necessary. Then they are to summarize what they heard each person say.

Discussion Questions:

1. Was it hard to be a good listener for five minutes?
2. Did you find your mind wandering while the other person was talking?
3. Did you need to ask many questions to keep the other person talking?
4. Do you think the other person thought you were very interested in what he/she had to say? How could you tell?

JOURNAL-ENTRY IDEAS

- Who is a very difficult person for you to listen to when he/she speaks? Why do you think this is so?
- You just won a contest—you have a private interview with anyone you want to talk to. Who would you select? What would you want him/her to talk about? What questions would you ask?

Name________________________________ Date ______________

What Do You Hear?

Worksheet #75

Directions: Seek out some of the following examples of individuals who may be a part of your life. Spend at least five minutes consciously listening to what they have to say. Do not be the first to initiate a conversation—listen. Then summarize what you have heard. What is on the mind of each person?

a parent: ______________________________

a brother/sister: ______________________________

someone in one of your classes whom you do not know very well:

____

a teacher: ______________________________

a neighbor: ______________________________

a waitress, clerk, salesperson: ______________________________

a bus driver: ______________________________

a friend (male): ______________________________

a friend (female): ______________________________

Lesson 55: "I can accept things about myself/my life that I cannot change."

Examples of Behavior:

Colored contacts in—
hair dyed and permed—$60
worth of cosmetics—tanned skin
from the booth—body-shaping
underwear—yeah, I can live
with myself.

—does not dwell on imperfections about self

—understands that some things are beyond one's control

—does not belittle self about shortcomings

—emphasizes positive attributes whenever possible

—does not blame self for situations that are not his/her fault

—"rolls with the punches"; recovers from setbacks

Desired Outcome:

Despite acknowledging his/her shortcomings or disabilities, the student will maintain a positive attitude about his/her life and self as evidenced by a healthy lifestyle.

Case Study:

Colm had been diagnosed with a severe learning disability in second grade. Reading and spelling skills were extremely difficult for him, although he could answer questions about what he had heard and had no problems with mathematics. By getting special help and spending time with a tutor, he learned how to compensate for these weak areas. In fact, he made up his own code for writing notes. No one else could understand what his scribbles and lines meant, but Colm had invented his own system for remembering things. His parents purchased a computer for him, and by learning to type and using a spellchecker, Colm was able to write papers for school. He always included beautiful drawings, graphs, or some sort of creative addition to his projects which made them even more interesting. Colm graduated from high school and was accepted to a college that provided special help for learning disabled students. He plans to be an engineer, which would incorporate his skills of mathematics and drawings. "I know I'm always going to have trouble reading," he admits. "I'm going to have to rely on a good computer and probably a good secretary," he laughs. "I'll make it."

Things to Try:

For the student

1. Learn as much as you can about your disabilities or problem situation.
2. Seek professional help when possible and necessary.
3. Find out about community organizations that may apply to you.
4. Learn how to make compensations for weak areas.
5. Talk to others in similar situations. What do they do?

For the teacher

1. Make adaptations as necessary for students with disabilities.
2. Allow students to use their strengths to produce projects, papers, and other assignments.
3. Give these students extra encouragement. They may have to work twice as hard as other students.
4. Assist students in making connections with agencies, counselors, or other people who may be helpful.

For the parent

1. Stay in close contact with your child's school, teacher, and principal; ask to be informed of progress and problems.
2. If possible, arrange for a tutor or volunteer to help your child.
3. Find out all you can about physical disabilities.
4. Be willing to arrange for family counseling, if necessary.

Activity #1: Case Study

Have students discuss Colm's situation. How did he compensate for his weak areas? How would this disability be similar to/different from a physical handicap? How did Colm take steps to improve a situation that is probably permanent?

Activity #2: Personal Application

Everyone has limitations. Have students work through ideas for accepting themselves and their limitations by using Worksheet #63, "Building Strengths."

Activity #3: Worksheet #76, I Have to Live with This!

Synopsis: By thinking about (and acknowledging) one's shortcomings or disabilities, an individual can begin to consciously make decisions as to how he/she will deal with them.

Directions: The student is to draw a picture or use words to depict a specific weakness or limitation of his/her life at present in two ways: on the left side, the student is to demonstrate the negative aspect of this situation; on the right side, the student is to show how he/she is overcoming or accepting the situation.

Discussion Questions:

1. Does everyone have some sort of limitation or situation that inhibits them from something? What are some examples?
2. How would being the child of an alcoholic, having AIDS, stuttering, or being in a wheelchair affect a person's ability to live the lifestyle of one's choice? How are these different situations perceived by the general public?
3. Does dwelling on a problem that cannot be changed make any difference? What could be done instead?
4. People have different ways of coping with their life problems. What are some examples of ways that are productive and ways that are pointless?

Journal-Entry Ideas

- Go through an ordinary day in your life. In what ways does your limitation affect what you do? What do you think would be different if this problem or situation suddenly disappeared?
- How has your limitation strengthened you? What are you able to do because of it? How has it affected your outlook on life?
- Pretend you are writing your life story as an old person. As you look back on your life, how could you see the problem or disability affecting the course of your life?

Name________________________________ Date ______________

I Have to Live with This!

Worksheet #76

Directions: Draw a picture below or use words to illustrate something about you or your life that you cannot change, even though you wish you could. On the left side, depict some of the drawbacks to this situation. On the right side, show how you have overcome (or are overcoming) the unpleasantness of this. Perhaps you have gained strength or sensitivity to others through this situation.

Positive Aspects

Lesson 56: "I like to learn and try new things."

Examples of Behavior:

—asks questions, is curious

—takes initiative to design and investigate new projects

—goes beyond the regular class assignment

—participates in sports, clubs, other groups

—uses free time constructively

—has a good imagination

Desired Outcome:

The student will select areas of interest and become involved in learning more about that interest area or participating in the activity.

Case Study:

Ellen had always been fascinated by the country of Spain. She had a pen-pal from Madrid when she was in elementary school. Her room was decorated with posters of bullfights, flamenco dancers, and castles. Ellen chose Spanish as her language to study in high school, and joined the Spanish club. Her dream was to be able to participate in a summer exchange program for six weeks. This was a school-sponsored program that was offered for students each summer. She and her parents figured out how much the trip would cost and decided to work together to save the money. Ellen became an active babysitter for the neighbors, cleaned several houses each week, and worked weekends at her father's office. That summer, Ellen was able to be an exchange student and go to Spain. When she returned, she realized how different and yet how similar the cultures were, especially for teenagers. "This summer has changed my life," she exclaimed. "I would love to go back. I would like to visit a lot of European countries. Who knows—maybe someday I'll be an ambassador to a foreign country! And it all started this summer!"

Things to Try:

For the student

1. Start keeping a file of things you are interested in—news articles, magazine photos, calendars, etc.
2. Watch educational television. You may be surprised at what's on!
3. Look through magazines at the library to get ideas to explore.
4. Visit a museum.
5. Look for opportunities to get involved in new activities (school clubs, church groups, volunteer programs, etc.).

For the teacher

1. Assign research projects that allow students to explore areas they are interested in.
2. Expose students to new ideas.
3. Work with art, music, and other specialty teachers to incorporate imagination and creativity into projects and lessons.
4. Find community volunteers to talk in your classroom about their hobbies (e.g., person who collects Civil War weapons, person who writes novels under a pen name, etc.).

For the parent

1. Try to work out a way for your child to have lessons, tutoring, etc., in interest areas (e.g., clean stalls at a local stable in exchange for riding lessons).
2. Have child make a list (and have it ready) of ten things he or she would like to do; then when "I'm bored, what can I do?" comes up, pull out the list.
3. Have your child research the idea if you have doubts about its safety (e.g., riding a motorcycle), and present his/her findings to you.
4. When your child is performing, be sure to make every effort to be there.

ACTIVITY #1: CASE STUDY

Have students discuss how Ellen's interest became a reality for her. What did it cost her in terms of money? time? effort? How did the experience affect her?

ACTIVITY #2: PERSONAL APPLICATION

Have students use Worksheet #63, "Building Strengths," to decide on ways they can encourage themselves to try things and to learn more about what interests them.

ACTIVITY #3: WORKSHEET #77, TRY THIS!

Synopsis: Students can become active participants in learning or trying something new.

Directions: Students are to read the items on the list and add appropriate items to it. They are to indicate which items they would be most interested in learning about. The rest of the project is up to them—to take the initiative to learn more about it.

Discussion Questions:

1. What did you select as an interest area that appeals to you?
2. How could you go about learning more about this?
3. What could you do to actively become a participant in this activity?
4. What's the time frame for accomplishing this? Could you actually get involved in this in the next few weeks or is this a far-off project?

JOURNAL-ENTRY IDEAS

- What would people think of you or say about you if you actually accomplished this goal? Do you think part of the reason that you'd like to do this is because of what other people would think?
- You made the headlines! Write a news article about yourself and what you learned or did. Look into the future if you have to . . .

Name______________________________ Date ____________

Try This!

Worksheet #77

Directions: Make a list of several things you have always wanted to learn about or try. It may not even be a possibility right now, but who knows! Put a star next to one or two that you think someday you might actually investigate.

parachuting out of an airplane

painting an oil painting

showing a cat at a show

learning to drive race cars

traveling to France

helping at a medical clinic in a third-world country

flying an airplane

cooking something very exotic

writing a novel

building a doghouse

rebuilding an old car

learning to photograph children

staying in a real castle in Europe

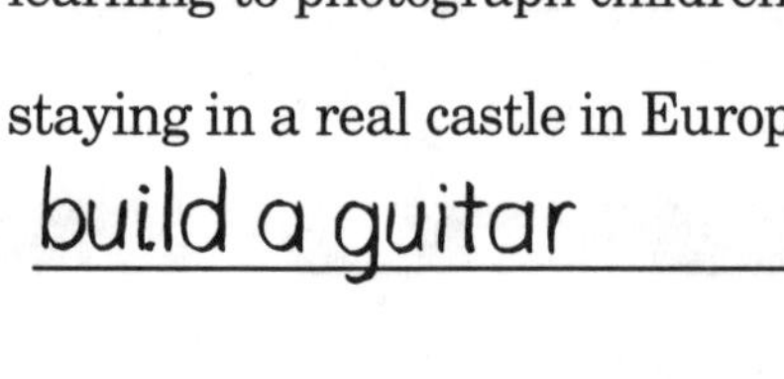

build a guitar

____

____

____

____

____

____

____

____

____

____

Lesson 57: "I can take constructive criticism."

Examples of Behavior:

Here, Mrs. Solsburg—
your formal evaluation.
Oh, thank you.
I can take it!

—asks for evaluation of work or projects

—uses ideas and suggestions from others

—is not offended or hurt when suggestions or criticism is given

—asks for clarification of suggestions

—doesn't assume his/her way is the best or only way

—seeks out alternative ways to complete projects

Desired Outcome:

When given constructive criticism or suggestions, the student will carefully consider and evaluate the ideas and incorporate them into making positive changes.

Case Study:

Myron was trying to make a working hurricane model for his science project. He had seen one at another school and thought it would be a great idea! After spending several days trying to figure out how to make it work, he just about gave up. Another boy who was in his science class, Tony, came up to him and said he realized he was having some trouble. "When I made one a few years ago at my other school," Tony said, "we used my mom's cappuccino maker to produce the steam. I think that might help your project." Myron thought about it for a minute. "I could try that," he said. "I think my aunt has one of those." Tony continued, "We also used a little house from my sister's dollhouse collection and busted the windows. We tipped it on its side to make it look like it had been blown around by the hurricane." Myron laughed. "Hey, that gives me an idea! I could put little red-and-white-striped socks under the house. It would look like it landed on a Wicked Witch!" He was getting excited about the new ideas he would use on his project.

Things to Try:

For the student

1. Ask others for their opinions.
2. Question others about reasons for their opinions.
3. Ask specifically, "What do you like/not like about this?"
4. If you disagree, plan NOT to argue your point.
5. Ask another person for a second, impartial opinion if you aren't sure you agree with the first one.

For the teacher

1. As you give criticism, be sure it is intended to be positive.
2. Have students critique projects, etc., as a group.
3. Give clear guidelines as to your expectations for assignments.
4. Have students brainstorm to come up with ideas to make a project interesting, visually attractive, creative, etc., before it is to be turned in.
5. Talk about the differences between constructive criticism and hurtful criticism.

For the parent

1. Talk with your child about your own experiences (at work, for example) of criticism and how it was delivered and received.
2. Model the attitude that "we can all improve ourselves."
3. When you give criticism to your child, preface it with remarks such as, "I'd like you to think about this," or "Do you think this would improve your idea?"
4. Explain that criticism is not necessarily a put-down, but an opportunity to make improvements.
5. Help your child separate the critical comments from the person giving the criticism; hopefully it is not a personal attack!

Activity #1: Case Study

Myron had a good idea for a science project, but got some assistance from another student to make improvements. Knowing that Tony only wanted to help, how could Myron use Tony's ideas? How could this have been an unpleasant situation if either Tony or Myron misunderstood the other's intentions?

Activity #2: Personal Application

Have students think about how they respond to constructive criticism. Using Worksheet #63, "Building Strengths," have them come up with ways they can be more open-minded to the constructive criticism of others.

Activity #3: Worksheet #78, Constructive Criticism

Synopsis: Comments of others can lead to making improvements in one's self or one's situation.

Directions: Students are to read the examples of constructive criticism given by individuals and state or write how they could potentially effect improvements in one's self or one's situation.

Discussion Questions:

1. Why do you think we sometimes resent having someone else tell us what to do or how to do something better?
2. Would you be more likely to listen to the comments of a friend or a stranger? What about a stranger who was a recognized expert in his/her field?
3. Do you think there are some people who simply enjoy criticizing others?
4. How could someone make constructive critical comments that come across as friendly and helpful, rather than demeaning? Are there certain "ways" to make words sound more acceptable?

Journal-Entry Ideas

- Give an example of a time when you or your work was criticized constructively by another person. Did you respect the person? Did you find the comments helpful? Did you make changes?
- Give an example of a time when you or your work was criticized in an unhelpful way by another person. How did you react to this type of criticism?
- If you were writing instructions for someone else as to how to give you constructive criticism, what would those instructions be? Do you really want to know the truth about something you are or have done?

Name____ Date ________________

Constructive Criticism

Worksheet #78

Directions: How are the following cartoons examples of people trying to tell you what to do in order to improve yourself, stay out of trouble, or teach you something?

Lesson 58: "Sometimes I do things simply because I know they are good for me."

Examples of Behavior:

—has a clear sense or direction about right and wrong

—aware of good health practices

—able to make decisions that promote good health

—desire to stay out of trouble

—does not spend a lot of time questioning; just does it!

—involved in sports and athletics

—takes care of appearance

Desired Outcome:

The student will make choices for him-/herself that reflect good health practices.

Case Study:

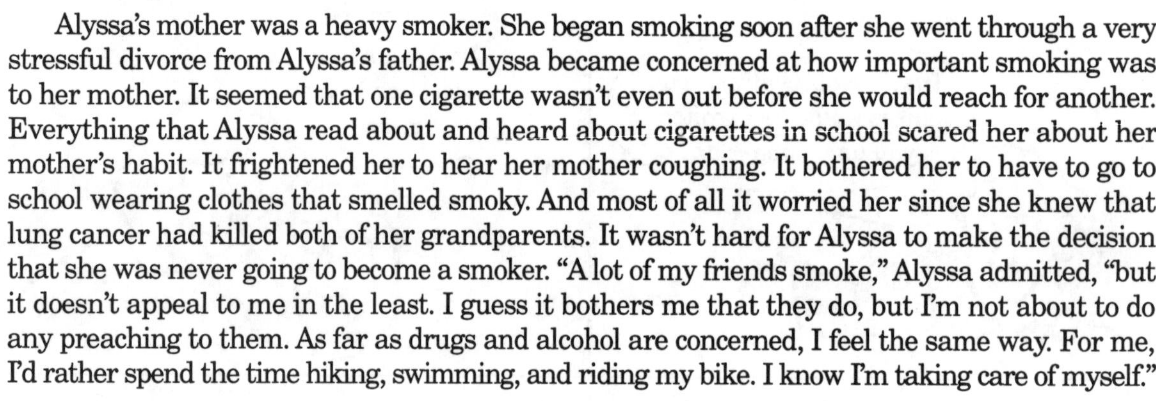

Alyssa's mother was a heavy smoker. She began smoking soon after she went through a very stressful divorce from Alyssa's father. Alyssa became concerned at how important smoking was to her mother. It seemed that one cigarette wasn't even out before she would reach for another. Everything that Alyssa read about and heard about cigarettes in school scared her about her mother's habit. It frightened her to hear her mother coughing. It bothered her to have to go to school wearing clothes that smelled smoky. And most of all it worried her since she knew that lung cancer had killed both of her grandparents. It wasn't hard for Alyssa to make the decision that she was never going to become a smoker. "A lot of my friends smoke," Alyssa admitted, "but it doesn't appeal to me in the least. I guess it bothers me that they do, but I'm not about to do any preaching to them. As far as drugs and alcohol are concerned, I feel the same way. For me, I'd rather spend the time hiking, swimming, and riding my bike. I know I'm taking care of myself."

Things to Try:

For the student

1. Go through a day trying to identify things that are good for you.
2. Look for opportunities to make choices that are in your best interests.
3. Shock your parents: resolve to eat more vegetables today.
4. Page through a health or fitness magazine; get some ideas.
5. Begin an exercise program.
6. Picture yourself healthier, more fit, and happier about yourself.

For the teacher

1. Teach nutrition and health whenever possible within your subject area.
2. Alert students to school organizations and other opportunities to participate in healthy activities.
3. Select and discuss news articles dealing with health.
4. Help students conduct and analyze surveys about student health habits.
5. When students must make a choice, help them learn to take the attitude: "Which choice is probably best for me?"

For the parent

1. Try to be more health-conscious at home.
2. Talk about decisions you have made in the interest of "doing the right thing."
3. Without being overbearing, mention sacrifices you or the family have made for a "greater good" or purpose.
4. Discuss with your child how these concepts can be good for you: self-denial, sacrifice, hard work, patience, turning the other cheek, unrecognized good deeds, delayed gratification, etc.

Activity #1: Case Study

Lead students in a class discussion about how and why Alyssa came to the decision that she did about smoking and other health-related habits. Do you think Alyssa may change her mind later? Do other students have the same convictions without having a parent who has struggled with this addiction?

Activity #2: Personal Application

Using Worksheet #63, "Building Strengths," have students identify ways they could make more decisions and better choices about what is good for them.

Activity #3: Worksheet #79, It's Good for You!

Synopsis: Identifying specific things that are good for a person is a first step toward making a commitment to begin incorporating them into one's life.

Directions: Students are to draw pictures to illustrate activities or events they consider to be "good" for them.

Discussion Questions:

1. What are some things that are good for you that are also easy for you to do?
2. What are some things that are good for you that are also difficult for you to do? Why?
3. Do you have any decisions or convictions about maintaining good habits based on an experience you or someone you are close to has had?
4. What are some ways advertising has helped promote good activities such as going to the dentist, losing weight, wearing a seat belt, etc.?

Journal-Entry Ideas

- Why can't chocolate-covered cherries be low-calorie? Why don't doctors tell you to get at least 12 hours of sleep each night? What are some things you enjoy that might have a "down side" to them?
- Make a promise to yourself to do (and continue) one activity simply because you believe it is good for you—even if you don't particularly enjoy it. What is it? How long can you stick with it? How do you feel about it and yourself?
- Pretend you have created the perfect food—good for you and tastes wonderful. Tell about it.

Name____ Date ______________

It's Good for You!

Worksheet #79

Directions: Draw a picture in each box below to illustrate something you might do simply because it is good for you. Then at the bottom of each box, write the specific area of your life (e.g., social, educational, religious, physical, etc.) that benefits from engaging in each activity.

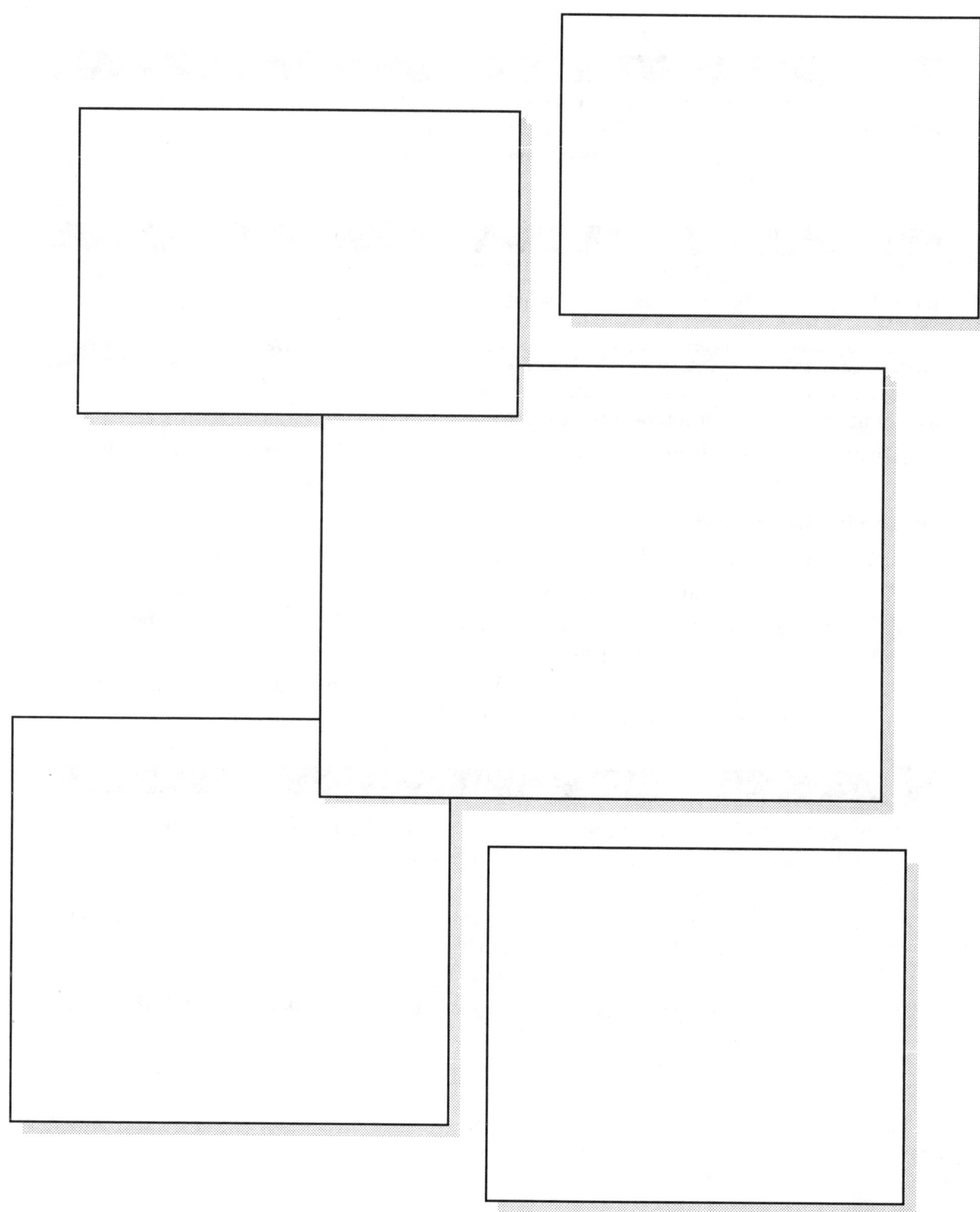

Lesson 59: "I have hopes and dreams."

Examples of Behavior:

—speaks of the future in optimistic terms

—has plans for the future

—looks forward to specific events

—takes steps to make future hopes possible

—not afraid to "dream big"

—bounces back when first plans may be thwarted or set back

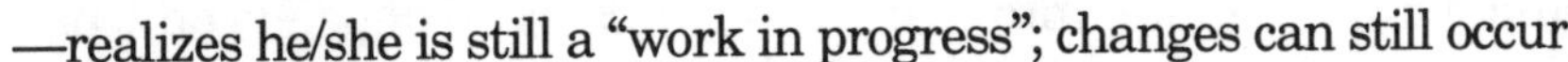

—realizes he/she is still a "work in progress"; changes can still occur

Desired Outcome:

The student will be able to identify several personal future goals that he/she intends to actively work towards achieving.

Case Study:

Kendi loved weekend days because he and his father always worked together in the workshop. Kendi's dad, an engineer, liked to work with wood and always had a project or two going in various stages of completion. Kendi would watch with fascination as his father carefully carved the face on a carousel horse that he was making. Each project took a long time, but both Kendi and his father enjoyed working together—sometimes without even saying a word to each other. As Kendi grew older, he became an informal apprentice to his father: learning various techniques of carving, using the hand tools, deciding which types of wood were suitable for various projects. Kendi entered projects of his own in the local 4-H fair—and usually received highest honors. "Someday I'm going to have a workshop even better equipped than my dad's," Kendi announced. "It was—and still is—a place where we can be together and really do something we both enjoy. I don't know if I will ever be as talented as my father, but maybe in time I'll be almost as good. Don't you think that kind of skill runs in the family? This is probably crazy, but I'd love to carve a huge totem pole and put it in my front yard someday!"

Things to Try:

For the student

1. Identify your hopes and dreams—write them down!
2. Don't let others discourage you or dissuade you from your dreams.
3. Acquire as much learning about your dream as you can.
4. Make it happen!

For the teacher

1. Share stories of people who achieved great hopes and dreams.
2. Provide a bulletin board for your students to display pictures or articles.
3. Highlight a "success story" each week.
4. Have students write a letter to themselves, date it, save it for a year, and then mail it to students.

For the parent

1. Find out what your child's hopes and dreams are.
2. Be a part of making it possible for your child to attain those hopes and dreams.
3. Don't worry about being harshly realistic—allow your child the chance to truly dream.

Activity #1: Case Study

Have students discuss how Kendi may have modeled his hopes and dreams from his father. Will his father be supportive of Kendi? How likely is it that Kendi will reach his dream?

Activity #2: Personal Application

Have students use Worksheet #63, "Building Strengths," to help identify some personal hopes and dreams.

Activity #3: Worksheet #80, Hopes and Dreams

Synopsis: Hopes and dreams can fall into many categories; it all depends on what the individual values. But it is important to begin to identify those hopes and dreams.

Directions: Using various media materials, students are to make a collage that depicts some semblance of their hopes and dreams.

Discussion Questions:

1. Do you think it is important for people to have hopes and dreams? Why?
2. What would the opposite emotion be like—if a person felt things were hopeless, unchanging, and without vision?
3. What things affect your life (e.g., inventions, policies) that are the result of someone else's dream?

Journal-Entry Ideas

- When did you first come up with a special hope or dream? Do you remember the circumstances involved?
- How realistic are you about your hopes for the future? Do you think it is possible you will achieve your hopes?
- Look into the future. Write about how you see a day in your "ideal" life!

Name____ Date ______________

Hopes and Dreams

Worksheet #80

Directions: Use pictures from magazines, photographs, original drawings, or any other medium to make a collage of your future dreams. You may want to incorporate several themes in your collage as well as a timeline—a dream for the next year, within 5 years, within 10 years, etc. When you have finished, be prepared to share your collage and its content with others.

Some ideas . . .

something you want to accomplish

a place you want to go

people in your life

your future family

changes you will see happen

changes you will make happen

what the world will be like

Lesson 60: "I can weigh the pros and cons of taking a risk and make a good decision."

Examples of Behavior:

—sees both sides of a situation
—draws conclusions of a given situation
—understands that "luck" can play a part in an outcome
—balances resources against the severity of the risk
—seeks advice
—makes a decision and "goes with it"

Desired Outcome:

Given an incomplete situation, the student will be able to weigh likely pros and cons of the situation, evaluate the risk factor, and make a decision.

Case Study:

Lynn wanted a car and was continually searching the classified ads, looking for something safe and affordable. Her father agreed to pay half of the car if she could find something he would approve. After weeks of looking and being disappointed, Lynn finally found something that seemed possible—an old sports car. It needed some work, but it was still flashy, very eye-catching, and fast. It had belonged to the college-bound son of a man who lived near them. The son had no trouble with the car, according to the man. Best of all, it was within Lynn's price range. "My dad was opposed to it right away," Lynn remembers. "He said I was distracted by the looks and didn't know that it was probably a lemon. Well, I knew I had some homework to do. I checked car magazines and found out that it was rated as highly reliable. I asked a friend of mine to recommend a reliable mechanic, who was willing to go out, see the car, drive the car, and give me a written list of what mechanical repairs would probably be necessary. I wasn't done yet—I knew my dad would look for cold, hard facts! Then I went to the bank and got an appraisal estimate of what the car was worth. Finally, I talked to the owner about providing me some kind of guarantee that the car was in reasonably good shape. Well, he wasn't willing to do that, and that concerned me. But, based on the other reports, I felt that I was willing to take a risk. And guess what? My dad was impressed with my arguments and put up half the money. I had a few repairs to pay for, but I'll tell you—I take good care of that car. And . . . I let my dad drive it once in awhile. It makes him feel good."

Things to Try:

For the student

1. Do your homework! Research all sides of a situation carefully!
2. Decide how much you are willing to lose in a risk.
3. Talk to responsible people about your situation.
4. Look for ways to get out from under a situation if things go wrong (make a back-up plan).

For the teacher

1. Point out pros and cons of situations as they come up in class.
2. Provide or fabricate situations in class occasionally for students to take risks and experience winning and losing.
3. Follow stories in the newspaper to examine risks that people have taken, the price, and the payoffs.

4. Assign students to conduct an informal survey of risks that students are willing to take. (Would you do X? Would you do Y? etc.)

For the parent

1. Instead of enforcing your opinion, assign your child the task of digging up facts about a situation first.
2. Be willing to examine the facts and be impartial.
3. Give examples from your own experience if your child will listen.
4. Ask your child to give you a written plan of his/her intentions, including back-up plans.
5. If you are providing collateral, get it in writing.
6. Sometimes you may have to make the best of a situation.

Activity #1: Case Study

Lynn organized and presented quite a case to her father—and won. What steps did Lynn take before taking the risk? How could things have turned out for Lynn if her father didn't like the car? What sources did she seek for facts? Did she have a back-up plan?

Activity #2: Personal Application

Using Worksheet #63, "Building Strengths," have students determine ways they could better assess and take risks in their lives.

Activity #3: Worksheet #81, Taking a Risk

Synopsis: Despite weighing the pros and cons of a situation, sometimes luck (good or bad) changes everything! One must be prepared to handle the amount of risk involved.

Directions: Students are given several hypothetical risks they must evaluate and decide on a course of action. To make it more interesting, several possible outcomes (unknown to students) are provided for each situation.

Discussion Questions:

1. What information would you want to seek for the first situation? Who would be able to give you this information?
2. What would be your back-up plan for the first situation?
3. What factors would you have to consider for the second example?
4. How important is the factor of trust in your friend and his/her judgment in the horse-racing situation?
5. What are some alternative plans to help you out in the late-for-work situation?
6. Have you known anyone who tried to use someone else's work for a grade? What happened?
7. How much of a factor is **luck** in any situation? Is there anything you have complete control over? If not luck, then what could affect a situation?

Journal-Entry Ideas

- List ten risky situations you have faced. How did they turn out?
- Many highly successful people have taken risks. What would you like to ask a highly successful person about the risks he/she has taken?
- Do you think it gets easier to take risks after you have been successful a few times? What could this lead to?

Name____ Date ________________

Taking a Risk

Worksheet #81

Directions: Which of the following risks would you take if you might gain the payoff? Then circle **a**, **b**, or **c** to find out what the outcome will be.

1. You have a very rare disease for which there is no cure. You can take an experimental medication that has side effects that make you feel dizzy, nauseous, and tired. You will have to make a trip to the hospital every other day to get a painful injection; however, the medication will control the progression of the disease. Do you want to try the experimental drug?

a **b** **c**

2. If you put $1,000 into a special money market, you can get a higher interest rate than if you just kept it in a savings account at the bank. However, you can't withdraw that money for a year or you'll lose the interest rate. Do you want to invest the money in a money market?

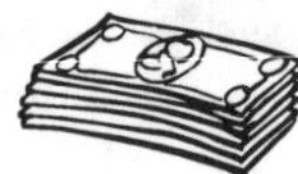

a **b** **c**

3. You are going to the race track and plan to bet $10. A friend gives you a tip—bet on the 99-1 horse in the fourth race. You can win a lot of money if the horse wins, and your friend says he has inside information that the horse will do well. In fact, he says you should bet at least $100. What do you want to do?

a **b** **c**

4. You're late for work! Your boss has warned you that if you come in later one more time—forget it! You're fired. You know that if you take the back country roads you can speed and possibly make it there on time. There aren't too many police officers out tonight. What will you do?

a **b** **c**

5. You have been studying for days to get through final exams. For your English final, you were supposed to have written a 10-page paper on an American author. You were just too tired to write it. Your older sister suggests you just copy a paper that was written by a friend of hers several years ago. She got an A on the paper and you probably won't get caught. Who would remember something from several years ago? Besides, it was a different teacher. What will you do?

a **b** **c**

Outcomes for Worksheet #81

Situation #1

a. The experimental drug has no effect on you whatsoever.

b. Your disease progresses quickly. Sorry!

c. The experimental drug works wonderfully and you have no symptoms at all. Meanwhile, a cure is discovered for your disease!

Situation #2

a. After you invest your money, another bank offers a similar deal with a much better interest rate.

b. You have a family crisis! You have to withdraw the $1,000 anyway and lose the interest.

c. You invest the money and collect a decent amount of interest.

Situation #3

a. You decide to play it safe. You bet $10 and the horse wins.

b. You bet $100 and the horse loses.

c. You bet $100 and the horse wins!

Situation #4

a. The police are out tonight. You get a speeding ticket AND you are late for work and lose your job.

b. You go along the country roads, speeding, and make it to work on time.

c. You have a flat tire on a back road and are late to work, but your boss understands and your job is safe!

Situation #5

a. The teachers are talking about the papers in the teachers' lounge and realize that the paper you turned in is someone else's. You get an F.

b. You copy the paper, turn it in, and get a B.

c. You decide to do your own work, turn in a late paper, and get a C.

Lesson 61: "I believe I do things that will make a difference."

Examples of Behavior:

—involved in social and/or political causes

—is interested in the world around him/her

—can take a leadership role

—states his/her opinions

—does not wait to take action; designs and carries out plans

—volunteers to be included

—generates ideas

Desired Outcome:

The student will become actively involved in issues that he/she believes are important.

Case Study:

Cedric was tired of looking at all the trash people threw into a vacant lot that most of the kids passed on their way to school. It was filled with beer bottles, leftover lunches, even old filthy articles of clothing, and other items that no one wanted to get close enough to identify. He thought it would make a great park or place to play some informal baseball. He complained to the school, the park department, and even city hall, but he didn't feel as though he was getting any answers. Finally, Cedric decided to take it upon himself to organize a group of kids to clean up the lot. He was almost surprised to find out how many kids felt the same way he did—in a matter of a few weekends the lot was cleaned up and kids were playing in it. Sadly, though, it was only a matter of time until people began dumping trash there again—it seemed like a hopeless task! Cedric got some support from adults in the neighborhood who signed a petition for more police to patrol the area. He attended a town council meeting with his concerns and, together with about 15 other concerned citizens, got the backing of the community. They began an informal Neighborhood Watch program. That, together with added police support, made a difference. "It mattered to me," Cedric explained. "I wanted a place where kids could play. Now there are even some flowers planted along one side of the fence. Next summer the city might put in a picnic table—imagine that! I was really happy that so many other people felt like I did. They just needed someone to get things going."

Things to Try:

For the student

1. Look around you; check out the posters on community bulletin boards—find out what people are excited/concerned about.
2. Start reading letters to the editor in your local paper.
3. Write a letter to the editor of your local paper.
4. Find out about a hospital/nursing home volunteer program.
5. Clean up a neighborhood.
6. Raise money for a worthy cause.
7. Do some chores for a senior citizen for free.

For the teacher

1. Alert students to community needs.
2. Organize interested students to tackle a specific project.

3. Assign students to research community volunteer groups. What do they do to help the community?
4. Have someone from your local Red Cross talk to your students.

For the parent

1. Support food drives, book fairs for causes, etc.
2. "Adopt" an elderly citizen, needy family, etc.
3. Encourage your child to invite a needy friend along when you go to a sports event, picnic, other place of interest.
4. Find out about church activities (food pantries, clothing and shelter needs, etc.); contribute as a family.
5. Convey the attitude to your child that he/she may not ever receive any recognition for his/her efforts; but that shouldn't matter!

Activity #1: Case Study

Have students trace the steps involved in Cedric's project to turn a vacant lot into a usable area for his community. Did everything go smoothly? What resources did Cedric use? What problems did he have to take into account? How will this experience affect Cedric in the future?

Activity #2: Personal Application

If students are interested in becoming active participants in their community, neighborhood, school, or other group, have them look over the ideas on Worksheet #63, "Building Strengths."

Activity #3: Worksheet #82, Change the World

Synopsis: There are many wrongs that need to be righted, causes that need a voice, and opportunities for people to make a difference—on all levels.

Directions: Students are to think of some situations or causes that are publicized on the local, state, national, and global levels. They are then to begin to identify ways they could become involved in making a difference in these causes.

Discussion Questions:

1. Have you or has your community been through a natural disaster (tornado, flooding, fire, etc.)? How did it draw the community together?
2. What fund-raising activities are common in your community?
3. How would you describe your community in terms of its receptiveness to helping each other out?
4. How much difference can one person make?

Journal-Entry Ideas

- If you had to pick one cause or situation you wish could be changed, what would it be? Why? How has this "hit home" or affected you?
- How would it make you feel if you were the designated recipient of someone else's goodness? Would you be embarrassed? Grateful? Would it depend on the situation?

Name____ Date ______________

Change the World

Worksheet #82

Directions: Look through a newspaper. What are some of the situations (local, state, national, worldwide) that you would like to see changed? Pick one at each level. What can you do to make a dent in the situation?

1. **a local situation:** ______________________________

2. **a statewide situation:** ______________________________

3. **a national situation:** ______________________________

4. **a world situation:** ______________________________

Lesson 62: "I can laugh at myself."

Examples of Behavior:

—does not take self overly seriously

—invites others to join in laughing at self

—sees the lighter side of situations

—alludes to weaknesses without putting self down

—doesn't maliciously laugh at others

Desired Outcome:

The student will demonstrate a good sense of humor in being able to laugh at him-/herself in many types of situations (embarrassing, formal, informal, etc.).

Case Study:

Connie was meeting some friends of the family at a restaurant. She hadn't seen these people in several years, but thought she would be able to recognize them. When she got to the restaurant, she stopped in the restroom, where she ran into her sister. "The Martins are sitting at the first table as you go into the main dining area," her sister told her. "Go ahead and join them—I'll be there in a minute." Connie went into the main dining area, located a familiar-looking family at the first table, introduced herself, and sat down. A lively conversation ensued, with them listening intently as Connie told them about her school activities, plans for the summer, and how good it was to see them all again. A few minutes later, her sister tapped her on the shoulder. "Our friends are sitting over there," she said, indicating a table further down. Connie looked up at a family waving at her. She blushed and exclaimed, "Oh, I'm so sorry! I thought you were somebody else!" The family laughed pleasantly and told her how much they enjoyed meeting her and hoped she had a pleasant summer, since it sounded as though she would be quite busy. All ended in laughter—mostly on Connie's part.

Things to Try:

For the student

1. Keep track of embarrassing moments; later it will be hilarious!
2. Share your embarrassing moments with a friend; do they seem so bad?
3. When you start to get down on yourself, think of how the situation could be humorous.
4. Resolve to laugh at yourself at least once a day.

For the teacher

1. When episodes happen in class, be sure not to laugh **at** a student; laugh **with** the student.
2. Tell students that you appreciate their good sense of humor.
3. Ask students to tell you the funniest thing that happened to them that week.
4. Laugh at yourself.

For the parent

1. Share an evening of looking at old family photographs and memories.
2. Do something fun together as a family; create a memory.
3. Tell your children anecdotes of what they did when they were little.
4. Create and maintain a family bulletin board.
5. Resolve to laugh together as a family at least once a day.

Activity #1: Case Study

Have students examine Connie's embarrassing moment. How could this have been a worse experience for Connie? How did the other people involved make it easier for Connie? How will she refer to this episode months from now?

Activity #2: Personal Application

Everyone has had embarrassing moments. Have students think through the ideas on Worksheet #63, "Building Strengths," to come up with ways to improve their ability to laugh at themselves.

Activity #3: Worksheet #83, A Good Laugh

Synopsis: Everyone has had an embarrassing moment. Being able to laugh at it and yourself is a healthy experience.

Directions: Students are to read the embarrassing anecdotes of people on the worksheet and think about how they could relate to or at least appreciate what happened.

Discussion Questions:

1. Do you enjoy being with people who can laugh at themselves? Do people who are constantly laughing at themselves make you feel uneasy? Why?
2. What is the difference between laughing **at** someone and laughing **with** someone? Who decides which direction the laughter should go?
3. How does the passage of time between the embarrassing moment and the present make things seem funnier or at least different? How does this add perspective to the event?

Journal-Entry Ideas

- What is your most embarrassing moment—the most awful thing you can remember? How does it make you feel today?
- Are you known for having a good sense of humor? Why/why not?
- When you do laugh at yourself, what do you focus on? A physical trait, habit, mannerism, etc.?
- Who is your favorite comedian—on television, movies, or other media? Why do you find this type of humor appealing?

Name________________________________ Date ______________

A Good Laugh

Worksheet #83

Directions: Think about a time when you had a good laugh at yourself. Perhaps at the time it wasn't so funny, but now that you look back, you realize everyone makes mistakes and you shouldn't have to take yourself so seriously all the time. Read the following examples; then be brave and share a good laugh on yourself.

Bonnie: I was interviewing for a job in a really nice office. I wanted to look good, so I borrowed my sister's dress. I was in a hurry, so I didn't bother to look at it carefully. The interview went well, but some of the people in the office were chuckling as I left. I couldn't figure out why. Well, when I got home, my sister asked me why I took that dress out of her closet. Didn't I notice the huge green stain on the back? Well, obviously, I didn't. I got the job despite looking pretty bad for my interview!

Mario: My parents had company one night and I didn't realize they were staying in the bedroom downstairs—right next to the bathroom I usually use. I'm sure they were intrigued while listening to me sing my morning shower songs. When I stepped out and saw them having coffee in the kitchen, they applauded me and wanted to know when my next concert was.

Aileen: There was a really cute guy working at the post office. He started flirting with me, and I was really losing my concentration. I was going to pick up a package for my parents and I was supposed to sign for it, but I was so nervous I forgot my address! All I could do was giggle. I'm sure he thought I was really stupid!

Tony: I was shopping at a department store with some friends—we were getting camping equipment and some sports stuff. I accidentally got the wrong cart and started to go through the checkout with a cart full of women's underwear and other embarrassing items. To make matters worse, the woman was a huge, loud person who accused me of taking her stuff. What would I want with her underwear?

Delilah: It was awful. My cousins were visiting and I had to take my boy cousin with me to a football game. He's a foot shorter than me, covered with pimples, and is a real dork. Everyone teased me about my new boyfriend. My history teacher was there and really thought I was going out with him. I couldn't make a scene in front of everyone—I just wanted to find a hole and crawl in!